Volume 9

The G. Stanley Hall Lecture Series

Archives of the History of American Psychology, Akron, Ohio

G. STANLEY HALL, 1844–1924

Volume 9

THE G. STANLEY HALL LECTURE SERIES

Edited by
Ira S. Cohen

1988 HALL LECTURERS

Laurel Furumoto
Carroll E. Izard
Martin E. P. Seligman
Michael J. Mahoney
Richard E. Mayer

AMERICAN PSYCHOLOGICAL ASSOCIATION

Published by the American Psychological Association, Inc.
1200 Seventeenth Street, N.W., Washington, DC 20036

ISBN: 1-55798-065-9
ISSN: 8756-7865

Copies may be ordered from:
Order Department
American Psychological Association
P.O. Box 2710
Hyattsville, MD 20784

Printed in the United States of America

CONTENTS

PREFACE

In 1980 the American Psychological Association, through its Committee on Undergraduate Education, initiated an annual lecture series, named the G. Stanley Hall Lecture Series in honor of the Association's first president, devoted to the needs of the undergraduate psychology instructor. At first, the focus was on the introductory psychology course—how to help the instructor keep abreast of the latest findings on the traditional topics of the course as well as the newer topics that continue to impose themselves on the up-to-date introduction to psychology.

In 1987 the scope of the series was broadened to include undergraduate teaching in general rather than the earlier, more limited emphasis on the introductory course. The series now included lectures that would update the materials in three of the topics usually included in undergraduate curricula, one on a relatively nontraditional topic, and one on some pedagogical aspect of undergraduate psychology teaching.

The 1988 Lectures followed this pattern. The three basic topics included one on emotions, by Carroll Izard; one on the history of psychology, by Laurel Furumoto; and one on clinical psychology, by Martin Seligman. The less traditional topic covered in this set of lectures was sport psychology, presented by Michael Mahoney. The series concluded with a lecture by Richard Mayer on the teaching of critical thinking. These lectures were well-attended and well-received at the APA annual convention in Atlanta, Georgia. In slightly modified form, they are reproduced here as Volume 9 of the G. Stanley Hall Lecture Series.

Psychologists who are experienced both as researchers and teachers in each of these five areas agreed to comment on earlier drafts of the manuscripts. As anonymous readers, these reviewers cannot be cited, but their help is gratefully acknowledged and some of their comments are interspersed in the descriptions that follow.

In the first chapter, Laurel Furumoto calls the attention of teachers of the history of psychology to the contemporary historiographic approaches that she refers to as the "new history" or "critical history." She first points out that the teaching of psychology's history has been marked by the "great man," "great ideas" approach, whereas sophisticated historiographic analyses have moved on to a study of the influences of institutions and of cultures on events and to analyses "from the bottom up" as well as "from the top down." Furumoto feels that these are changes in the mode of scholarship that are only now beginning to influence the study of the history of psychology.

After describing the new history and its stirrings in the history of science and, more particularly, the history of psychology, she then presents women's history as an illustration of this new scholarship. From there she moves to examples from her own work on Mary Whiton Calkins, an early (1905) president of the American Psychological Association. Furumoto shows how a consideration of gender-specific themes, derived from archival research, leads to a different understanding of Calkins' career than that which might be disclosed by a more traditional approach to history. A significant feature of this chapter is Furumoto's description of a history of psychology seminar which serves as an example of integrating the new history into the undergraduate course. She has done a truly impressive job of articulating the ideals of the new history and making these issues understandable to the teachers of the history of psychology, most of whom have no detailed involvement in research in the field.

In the second chapter, Carroll Izard points out that the theories of emotions can be divided into two broad categories: biosocial and cognitive-social. The biosocial theories assume that emotions are biologically and genetically based, only subsequently to interact with learned factors like social roles. The cognitive-social theories assume that emotions derive from interactions with the environment and our appraisal of it. Izard's approach is primarily biosocial, but he provides frequent explanations of the contrasting views of cognitive-social theorists. He covers the contemporary approaches to the study of emotions by relating these theories to five significant issues: (a) emotion activation, or the cause of an emotion; (b) the structure, or component parts, of emotions; (c) the functions of emotions; (d) the interrelationships of emotions, motivation, and adaptation; and (e) the relation of emotions to such factors as temperament and personality.

Few people are as knowledgeable about theory and research on emotions as is Izard. In this chapter he provides the undergraduate instructor with an interesting and clearly written, updated and informed account of contemporary thinking about this rapidly growing area of psychology.

In the following chapter, Martin Seligman provides a case illustration of research in clinical psychology by addressing the question, Why is there so much depression today? He begins by pointing out that the rate of depression among contemporary Americans is much higher—perhaps ten times higher—now than years ago, and proceeds to offer epidemiological and anthropological evidence in support of this finding. He then argues that this change is due to an increase in individualism in modern (post-World War II) American society concomitant with a diminished involvement with the larger, supporting institutions (family, religion, country) that can be referred to as the "commons." Taken together, he continues, this results in individuals particularly vulnerable to depression, a disorder of learned helplessness when the self is thwarted—"individuals, preoccupied with their own hedonics, who take the ordinary failures of life badly and have few larger beliefs to fall back on. . . . " The resolution to this dilemma, he suggests, is certainly not to escape from the freedoms that individualism brings, but rather "to strike a healthier balance between commitment to the self and to the common good."

Seligman's chapter is well-written and thought-provoking. It is certain to be a source of discussion and debate among teachers and students, who might wish to compare Seligman's resolution to the metaphor proposed by Arthur Schopenhauer, the 19th century German philosopher. Schopenhauer likened the human condition, with its need for individualistic expression and its often incompatible need for social support and community, to the case of shivering porcupines. They desire warmth, but closeness brings pain. They accommodate, Schopenhauer says, by setting themselves far enough apart so as not to prick each other, yet close enough to avoid freezing . . . and they shiver.

In the fourth chapter, Michael Mahoney, himself a world-class weightlifter, surveys the newly recognized field of sport psychology and some of its important current developments. The professional and scientific contributions of sport psychology are first presented in a historical context. Mahoney then reports on the personality studies of exceptional (world-class) athletes and on the psychological skills that enhance athletic performance—anxiety management, concentration skills, confidence, motivation, and mental preparation.

Mahoney points out that at the 1976 Olympics in Montreal, swimming gold-medalist Mark Spitz commented that at that level of competition, "physical differences are minimal relative to the importance of mental factors." It is these psychological factors and their application in the realms of recreation and athletics that Mahoney addresses in an interesting, well-written, and logically organized chapter.

In the final chapter, Richard E. Mayer presents three examples of programs that have been shown to improve the way students think, that is, "to take what they learned and successfully use it in new situations." One program demonstrates structure training as applied to scientific thinking: a second program demonstrates representation training applied to mathematical thinking; and the third shows conceptual-model training applied to simple computer programming. These programs are based on "teaching small, component skills rather than viewing intellectual performance as based on a single, monolithic ability" and approach the teaching of thinking through specific subject matter domains rather than as a separate domain-free topic. Mayer adds some intriguing ideas on how teaching thinking skills might be adapted within the domain of psychology. The studies he describes are interesting and well-executed. The chapter is a well-written, clear description of a practical approach to the teaching of thinking.

Each year the APA's Committee on Undergraduate Education selects outstanding psychologists for the following year's G. Stanley Hall Lecture Series, keeping in mind the criteria of teaching effectiveness as well as subject matter expertise. The committee charged with the selection of the lecturers whose papers appear in this volume included Antonio E. Puente, Margaret A. Lloyd, Margaret S. Martin, Janet R. Matthews, and Mark E. Ware. Their efforts are gratefully acknowledged.

Finally, thanks are due to Genevieve Whittemore, who handled most of the early correspondence with the authors, and to ChiChi Sileo, who helped with the arrangements for the presentation of the lectures at the 1988 convention. I also wish to express my appreciation to Donna Stewart, the managing editor who supervised this volume through the editing process; and to Susan Bedford, the technical/production editor who prepared most of the manuscripts for publication.

Ira S. Cohen

LAUREL FURUMOTO

THE NEW HISTORY OF PSYCHOLOGY

Laurel Furumoto is professor of psychology at Wellesley College, where she has been on the faculty since 1967. Her interest in the history of psychology reaches back to her graduate school days at Ohio State University where she earned an MA degree in clinical psychology, and at Harvard University where she took her PhD degree in experimental psychology. Soon after her arrival at Wellesley, Furumoto began investigating the life and career of one of her predecessors on the faculty there, Mary Whiton Calkins (1863-1930), who was an eminent psychologist in her own time but was largely overlooked by modern historians of the field.

In the mid-1970s, Furumoto began a fruitful collaboration with historian of psychology Elizabeth Scarborough, which led to a coauthored volume published in 1987 by Columbia University Press entitled *Untold Lives: The First Generation of American Women Psychologists.* A Fellow of the American Psychological Association's History Division and the Division on the Psychology of Women, Furumoto is currently serving on the APA Task Force on Centennial Celebrations, created by the Board of Directors to coordinate activities commemorating the hundredth anniversary of the association in 1992.

LAUREL FURUMOTO

THE NEW HISTORY OF PSYCHOLOGY

Psychologists currently teaching the history of their discipline are unlikely to have had any instruction in the field other than a graduate level course introducing them to "great men" and "great ideas." This stands in marked contrast with psychologists teaching courses in areas such as personality, developmental, social, and experimental psychology, where prior training in research methods, as well as in the subject matter of the specialty, is the norm.

This lack of training in historiographical methods can be attributed to the fact that, up until approximately 20 years ago, history of psychology was a neglected research area. Recently, the situation has changed; we are now witnessing a surge of historical scholarship that deserves to be called "the new history of psychology." However, with a few exceptions (see Benjamin, 1988; Hilgard, 1987; Leahey, 1987), textbooks in the history of psychology have yet to reflect the advent of this new history, and most teachers of the history course, not trained as historians, are heavily dependent on such works for their approach to the topic.

An almost inevitable conclusion follows: The history of psychology as currently taught in the typical college and university classroom remains largely uniformed by the new history, a state of affairs that, in my view, affords our students an impoverished understanding of psychology's past. In this chapter, I want to argue for a change in the status quo by drawing the attention of teachers of the history course to the new history and by discussing its implications for transforming the traditional history of psychology course.

Rise of the New History

Within the discipline of history proper, the so-called "new history" is not all that new; in fact, it dates back at least to 1912. In that year, a collection of essays appeared by James Harvey Robinson (1912), professor of history at Columbia University, entitled *The New History*. In this volume, Robinson made a plea for the adoption of what he called "the modern historical outlook." Instead of "perpetuating the conception of history as a chronicle of heroic persons and romantic occurrences" (p. 10), which he dubbed the "epic poem approach," Robinson advocated the study of institutions as a surer route to historical understanding. Robinson considered institutions to be synonymous with national habits, and he defined them "in a very broad sense, to include the ways in which people have thought and acted in the past, their tastes and their achievements in many fields besides the political" (p. 15).

In the ensuing three quarters of a century, the new history has become increasingly influential within the profession. It has also become increasingly diverse. The term "new history" as it is currently used refers to a variety of approaches, such as social history, psychohistory, and cliometrics, that are not necessarily consistent with one another, but which have in common the fact that they all represent a challenge to traditional history. The dominant place that the new history now occupies is testified to in a recent assessment of its status by Gertrude Himmelfarb (1987), a well-known historian who places herself in the camp of the old history. In fact, Himmelfarb claims that the new history has largely displaced the old, moving it from the center to the periphery of the profession.

The new history has long made its presence felt within the specialty area of history of science as well. Thomas Kuhn (1968) described how, over the course of the 20th century, historians of science gradually went through a reorientation in the way they viewed their subject matter. Efforts in the history of science were unevenly distributed, however, as Kuhn notes, and until fairly recently were almost exclusively confined to the physical and biological sciences. Thus, Kuhn could observe as late as 1968 that "as yet, the new historiography has not touched the social sciences" (p. 77).

In the mid-1970s, another historian of science, Stephen J. Brush (1974), published an article in the journal *Science* with the provocative title, "Should the History of Science Be Rated X?" At the outset, he acknowledged that the history he was referring to was primarily that of physics and early astronomy, as "these subjects usually furnish the successful examples of the scientific approach to be emulated in other fields" (p. 1164). Brush debated the pros and cons of teaching the new history of science to science students, indicating certain dilemmas that it posed for instructors who wanted to incorporate the historical perspective into their courses. For example, he pointed out that whereas traditional history portrayed the scientist as an objective fact finder and neutral observer, the new history emphasized the notion that scientists often operate in a subjective fashion, under the influence of a variety of extra-scientific factors. Also, Brush claimed, the new history rejected the traditional view of scientific activity as a continuous progression from error to truth, and opted instead for a model that depicts scientific change as a shift from one world view to another—world views that are linked to theoretical commitments involving esthetic as well as metaphysical considerations.

These aspects of the new history of science, Brush observed, fly in the face of the canons of scientific method as typically taught to science students and run counter to the beliefs of most of their science teachers as well. Teachers who want "to indoctrinate students in the traditional role of the scientist as a neutral fact finder," he concludes, "should not use historical materials of the kind now being prepared by historians of science" (p. 1170) because they will not serve the purpose well.

If, as I have attempted to document thus far, history in general, including the subfield of history of science, has been profoundly altered by the new history's coming of age, what has its impact been within the history of psychology? As previously mentioned, just 20 years ago Kuhn (1968) could see no influence of the new historiography in the social sciences. At about the same time another historian of science, Robert Young (1966) published a lengthy paper evaluating the status of scholarship in the history of the behavioral sciences. Young had few kind words for and many criticisms of the work then being done in the history of psychology. In particular, he took historians of psychology to task for stressing "the history of problems of current interest" and for then proceeding to write history "backwards from the viewpoint of the modern textbook" (p. 18). Young charged that historians of psychology in the mid-1960s remained largely unaware of the message of the new historiography of science and demonstrated "little grasp of the implications of the demand that we understand the past in its own terms before comparing it with our own vantage point" (p. 19).

Young also reviewed the history of psychology as written by psychologists in the previous four decades, pointing out its shortcomings. For one, the field appeared to him to be severely afflicted by what he termed "perseveration." As Young described it, "the number of subjects within the history of behavioural sciences which would repay intensive study, seems inexhaustible" (p. 26). Yet, he noted, the same stories are being told time and again. In addition to the shortcoming of perseveration, Young identified "three limitations from which the history of psychology suffered: great men (whom to worship?), great insights, and great dates" (p. 36). In spite of his predominantly negative assessment of the status of historical scholarship in psychology in the mid-1960s, Young's review concluded on an optimistic note. The appearance of the *Journal of the History of the Behavioral Sciences,* which had begun publication in 1965, he hailed as "the single most important development in the field, which gives hope for the future" (p. 36).

There were several other developments in 1965 and shortly thereafter that established the history of psychology as a legitimate subfield. See Watson (1975) for a detailed account of these events. In September 1965, the American Psychological Association's Council of Representatives approved the formation of the Division of the History of Psychology, Division 26; and in November of that year, the Archives of the History of American Psychology were officially established at the University of Akron. In 1967, the first graduate program in the history of psychology was launched at the University of New Hampshire in the Department of Psychology under the direction of Robert I. Watson. The following year, New Hampshire hosted the first National Science Foundation institute on the teaching of history of psychology. The 6-week summer program brought together 30 participants and 7 lecturers and spawned an organization, Cheiron, the International Society for the History of the Behavioral and Social Sciences. Conceived in the summer of 1968 by the members of the institute as a means of perpetuating the group, the Cheiron society began its annual meetings in 1969.

The New History Comes to Psychology

For a decade or so following these events, work in the history of psychology was dominated by the traditional approach to the history of science. That is, history was written by practitioners of the discipline, who by and large viewed the history of science as a cumulative linear progression from error to truth and who tended to write history backwards from the present, concentrating on "great men" and "great ideas." The mid-1970s witnessed a change as the new history made its appearance within the history of psychology, challenging traditional scholarship. The challenge issued from some psychologists who had come to specialize in historical scholarship and some historians of science who had begun to study the social sciences.

The new history, known as "critical history" to some of its advocates, would perhaps be more accurately called new or critical *histories* in that it has assumed a variety of forms within intellectual as well as social history. One focus of the new scholarship in intellectual history has been a reexamination of the work of Wilhelm Wundt, the traditional founding father of experimental psychology. As the 1979 centennial of his Leipzig laboratory approached, historians of psychology began to read Wundt's works in the original, discovering, in the words of one historian (Ash, 1983), "a philosopher and scientist quite different from the one portrayed in standard histories" (p. 169). A leader in the reappraisal of Wundt's thought, cognitive psychologist Arthur L. Blumenthal (1975), observed that Wundt scholars in the 1970s were "in fair agreement that Wundt as portrayed today in many texts and courses is largely fictional and often bears little resemblance to the actual historical figure" (p. 1081). Nor, Blumenthal went on, was this "only the nit-picking of a few antiquarians obsessed with minor matters of interpretation" (p. 1081). On the contrary, he asserted, "these are claims about the very fundamentals of Wundt's work, often asserting the opposite of what has been a standard description prevailing over much of the past century" (p. 1081).

The revisionist Wundt scholars tend to consider the source of this pervasive misrepresentation of Wundt's thought to be his student E. B. Titchener (Blumenthal, 1975, 1980; Danziger, 1979, 1980; Leahey, 1981; Tweney & Yachanin, 1980). An explanation for the subsequent spread of the distorted view can be found in Kurt Danziger's (1979) observation that E. G. Boring's classic *A History of Experimental Psychology* (1950) fails utterly to convey Wundt's vision of psychology. Danziger notes that "it is very difficult to reconcile Boring's interpretation of Wundt's fundamental ideas with the original work, especially the larger and most important part of the original which remains untranslated. This is not really surprising. It is apparent that Boring took his admired teacher, E. B. Titchener as a guide in these matters, and Titchener practically made a career out of interpreting Wundt in his own highly idiosyncratic fashion" (Danziger, 1979, p. 206).

The work of such Wundt scholars represents part of a larger movement by intellectual historians of psychology toward meticulous investigation of original sources. An important institutional locus for this brand of new scholarship is the University of New Hampshire, where Robert I. Watson's successors, David E. Leary and William R. Woodward, carry out their own research and teach history of psychology to both graduate and undergraduate students. Woodward (1980) described the effort there as "a critical approach to knowledge—involving the pursuit of limited goals in keeping with modern historical scholarship, awareness of and compensation for sources of bias in the history of science, and a sensitivity to the social function of this young cross-disciplinary field, the history of psychology" (p. 52). One historian of science (Ash, 1983) characterized the New Hampshire program as "clearly not intended to radically alter psychology, but to help it enrich its knowledge of itself by professionalizing its historiography" (p. 172). Three recently published volumes, *A Century of Psychology as Science* (Leary & Koch, 1985), *The Problematic Science: Psychology in Nineteenth Century Thought* (Woodward & Ash, 1982), and *Psychology in Twentieth Century Thought and Society* (Ash & Woodward, 1987), testify to the steps the program is taking in this direction.

Another domain of scholarship in the new history of psychology is that of social history. A focus for some of this work is the neglect of contributions made by groups other than White males in the history of psychology. Examples of this approach include Robert V. Guthrie's (1976) book *Even the Rat Was White,* which provides an account of Black psychologists in America; a paper by Maxine D. Bernstein and Nancy Felipe Russo (1974), calling attention to contributions of women psychologists; and an article that I published on the life and career of the first woman president of the American Psychological Association, Mary Whiton Calkins (Furumoto, 1979).

Also fitting into the category of social history is a body of work that adopts a critical stance toward the discipline of psychology itself, rather than being primarily concerned with history's oversights; see, for instance, Buss (1979). An early, often-cited example of this genre is a paper by Franz Samelson (1974), a social psychologist, in which he called upon his colleagues to engage in a critical examination of their past. Samelson's paper debunked the notion conveyed by many recent social psychology textbooks that Auguste Comte was the founder of modern social psychology. Identifying Gordon Allport (1968) as the likely source of this idea, Samelson used Allport's presentation of Comte as "a strategically located example," going on "to open up some basic issues concerning the past and present history of social psychology, the treatment of history at the hands of psychologists, and the meanings and functions of such histories" (Samelson, 1974, p. 217).

Samelson argued that Allport was highly selective in his use of Comte's ideas, presenting those that appeared consonant with modern social psychology and disregarding the rest, many of which were incompatible or even antithetical to it. "Such treatment of history," Samelson concluded, "amounts not to a *critical examination* of the past, but to the creation of an origin myth" (pp. 222-223). The function of such origin myths, in Samelson's opinion, is to validate and legitimize present ideas by demonstrating their venerability. That is, if it can be shown that a great thinker held these views a hundred years ago, an impression of continuity and tradition accrues to the discipline. Samelson took pains to point out that it was not his objective "to attack Allport's integrity as a scholar, but to call attention to the naivete with which psychologist historians approached the history of their discipline" (p. 223).

Works in the history of psychology, Samelson charged, typically revealed a lack of any real awareness of recent developments in the field of history of science. This scholarly discipline, Samelson explained, no longer sees "its task as producing chronicles of scientific discoveries, or biographical accounts of its heroes, or the settling of priority claims. A new sensitivity for historical material has developed. It insists on respecting the integrity of the thought of past figures, on the need to understand them in their own terms, within their historical context, instead of mapping out straight lines of scientific progress or pointing to anticipations of the present" (Samelson, 1974, pp. 223-224).

Echoing Kuhn's (1968) and Young's (1966) verdicts, Samelson (1974) maintained that the new historiography of science had not reached the social sciences. He found it rather odd that psychologists, who were so proud of methodology in their own field, showed so little awareness of methodological issues in their approach to historical work. Issuing a warning that "a science without memory is at the mercy of the forces of the day," Samelson voiced the opinion that "the history of social psychology as a critical examination of the past, leading to a better understanding of the present, still remains to be written" (p. 229).

Samelson's (1974) appeal for a more critical history, which had appeared in an obscure journal, was answered in the principal professional journal of the American Psychological Association in the latter half of the 1970s. Several articles and commentaries bearing the stamp of this brand of critical history appeared in the *American Psychologist* between 1976 and 1980. They began with a series of two papers by another social psychologist, Lorenz J. Finison (1976, 1978) discussing the impact and consequences of unemployment among psychologists during the Depression. Drawing on interviews and archival materials, Finison reconstructed attempts by psychologists to alleviate the unemployment situation. He focused on two organizations that resulted from these attempts, the Society for the Psychological Study of Social Issues and the Psychologists League, carefully placing them in their historical and sociopolitical context.

Two more critical history papers, one by Ben Harris, a social personality psychologist, and another by a historian of science, John O'Donnell, appeared in 1979. Harris' paper was a reexamination of John B. Watson and Rosalie Rayner's (1920) classic study of conditioned emotional responses in the infant Albert B. The attempt to condition little Albert, Harris observed, was widely used in undergraduate textbooks "to illustrate the applicability of classical conditioning to the development and modification of human emotional behavior" (Harris, 1979, p. 151). However, a careful reading of these accounts, Harris noted, reveals extensive distortion and misrepresentation of the original experiment. This, combined with the fact that the Albert study, due to its many methodological flaws, was not very convincing proof of classical conditioning of emotional behavior, raises the question of what function the story serves.

Harris sees the Albert study as another example of what Samelson, in discussing Comte as the alleged father of social psychology, called an origin myth. And, speaking more generally, he argued that "modern citations of classic studies can often be seen as attempts by current theorists to build a false sense of continuity into the history of psychology" (p. 157). This myth-making process, Harris emphasized, is not a conscious attempt to defraud. Rather, it stems from the attempt to build historical support for new theoretical perspectives. As for the problem with such reevaluations, Harris, in agreement with Samelson, concluded that "they obscure the actual factors that determine the course of scientific research" (p. 157).

The paper by O'Donnell (1979) is an account of historian of psychology E. G. Boring, focusing on the 1920s and examining "the extent to which Boring's professional concerns affected his historical vision" (p. 289). O'Donnell portrayed Boring as "a staunch experimentalist," dedicated to the ideal of pure research, who became increasingly disturbed by "what he perceived to be a pernicious tendency toward applied psychology after World War I" (p. 289). In fact, O'Donnell observed, "power had shifted significantly to the proponents of applied psychology after the war" (p. 289). This, coupled with dwindling institutional support for psychological laboratories, inability to attract and place future experimentalists, and established experimentalists going over to applied work, "fortified Boring's fears for the future of psychological research in America and fueled his resentment of applied psychology" (p. 292).

O'Donnell contends that if Boring had not considered history a forceful persuader, he would not have absented himself from the laboratory to take up historical work during what was potentially the most productive period of his career. And, he asserts, "for Boring, history was not merely a matter of describing the past but of altering the future" (p. 289). O'Donnell suggests that Boring's intent in writing *A History of Experimental Psychology* (1929) was to make experimentalism more visible while downplaying the impact of applied concerns in the development of the discipline. O'Donnell characterizes the resulting history as one that delineates "the intellectual *content* but not the social *function* of psychology in America" (p. 289). Maintaining that, in this respect, subsequent historiography of psychology has followed Boring's lead, O'Donnell calls for a change: "beneficiaries of Boring's immense erudition, we must not remain prisoners of his perspective" (p. 294).

In 1980, additional discussion of the historiography of psychology made its way into the pages of the *American Psychologist.* Several reactions to Harris' little Albert paper (1979) appeared in the comment section (Cornwell, Hobbs, & Prytula, 1980; Church, 1980; Murray, 1980; Seligman, 1980) together with a reply from the author. Harris (1980) began his remarks by addressing various issues raised in the published responses to his paper and concluded by drawing a distinction between what he called "ceremonial" and "critical" history, urging historians of psychology to do less of the former and more of the latter. Harris defined ceremonial history as "accounts without a critical focus, stories (or cautionary tales) that have a symbolic function but do not help us understand the social forces with which we interact daily" (p. 219). By contrast, a "socially informed, critical history of psychology," Harris argued, is a better method, which instead of focusing on the personal characteristics and intentions of historical figures, such as J. B. Watson, for example, asks "*historical* questions about subjects such as Watson's career, the acceptance of behaviorism in American psychology, and its subsequent institutionalization" (p. 219). Fortunately, Harris noted, workers in the history of psychology were beginning to address the issue of "what constitutes a good historical question" (p. 219).

One of these workers, Franz Samelson, whose call as early as 1974 for a more critical history of psychology has already been discussed, was the author of another paper on the topic that appeared in the *American Psychologist* in 1980. Samelson cited Harris' recently published paper on little Albert, juxtaposing Watson and Rayner's study (1920) with the identical-twin study of English psychologist Cyril Burt (1966) "in order to raise some questions about their status and treatment in the social process of (psychological) science" (Samelson, 1980, p. 619). Observing that "serious historical research may have unexpected outcomes" (p. 622), Samelson pointed to L. S. Hearnshaw's study of Burt. Hearnshaw (1981) writes in the preface to his biography that when he agreed to undertake it, it had never occurred to him to suspect Burt's integrity; yet, by the time the book was completed, Hearnshaw was convinced that the charges of fraud made against Burt after his death in 1971 were true.

Thus Samelson (1980) notes, with a touch of irony, that in 1979, as the Wundt and Watson centennials were showing "the ceremonial function of history at its best" (p. 622), historical work in a more critical vein was calling into question the scientific bases of two major opposing psychological paradigms. On one hand, there was the charge that Burt had falsified data on identical twins reared apart, evidence that had been used in arguments for the heritability of intelligence. On the other hand, there was the claim that there were serious methodological flaws in Watson's study of little Albert, "the textbook exemplar for human conditioning" (Samelson, 1980, p. 622).

"What are we to make of such allegations?" (p. 622), Samelson asks. Noting that it would be easy to focus on the actors and their intentions in fashioning an explanation (e.g., Watson was more a propagandist than a scientist), Samelson argues that ultimately this approach amounts to an evasion. The real question, in Samelson's view, is why it took so long for this public criticism to surface when "anybody who read Watson's accounts carefully and critically, could not fail to see some problems," and "anybody reading through Burt's papers in similar manner could not fail but be struck by the implausibility of some of his stories" (p. 623). Could it be, Samelson asks, that there "is a shared hesitancy to look back at what we are really doing, an attitude of encouraging public criticism to go only so far and not to touch fundamentals?" (p. 624). Admitting that an answer to this question was clearly beyond the scope of his paper, Samelson noted that the mere fact that it presents itself "indicates at least the need for a more critical understanding of our history and, more generally, for a more reflexive and self-critical attitude toward our activities" (p. 624).

Whereas the decade of the 1970s witnessed the stirring of the new history of psychology, the 1980s has seen an outpouring of the new scholarship (e.g., Ash & Woodward, 1987; Burnham, 1988; Capshew & Lazlo, 1986; Danziger, 1985; Finison, 1986; Harris, Unger, & Stagner, 1986; Leary, 1987; Leary & Koch, 1985; Morawski, 1986, 1988; Napoli, 1981; O'Donnell, 1985; Pauly, 1986; Samelson, 1985; Scarborough & Furumoto, 1987; Sokal, 1987; Walsh, 1985; Woodward & Ash, 1982). What can be said in general about the characteristics of this new history and how it differs from the old? I see at least five noteworthy aspects: The new history tends to be critical rather than ceremonial, contextual rather than simply the history of ideas, and more inclusive, going beyond the study of "great men." The new history utilizes primary sources and archival documents rather than relying on secondary sources, which can lead to the passing down of anecdotes and myths from one generation of textbook writers to the next. And finally, the new history tries to get inside the thought of a period to see issues as they appeared at the time, instead of looking for antecedents of current ideas or writing history backwards from the present content of the field.

My Encounter With the New History

To illustrate in concrete terms how the traditional and the new history differ, I want to describe to you my own experience in teaching and doing research in the history of psychology, and more specifically my intellectual pilgrimage from the old to the new history of psychology. This personal case study extends back over more than 25 years to the time when I was a graduate student. In the early 1960s, while completing a PhD in experimental psychology at Harvard, I learned about psychology's "great men" and their "great ideas" from both R. J. Herrnstein and emeritus professor E. G. Boring.

My first step away from this traditional approach consisted of looking beyond "great men" to the "great women" in the history of psychology. In the decade of the 1970s, my initial research in history focused on rediscovering Mary Whiton Calkins, a predecessor of mine at Wellesley College, and forgotten fourteenth president of the APA back in 1905. In addition to reintroducing Calkins to late twentieth-century psychologists by giving talks and publishing accounts of her life and career, I called attention to her contributions, most notably the invention of the paired-associate technique for the study of memory, and a system of self-psychology.

A further departure from traditional history has characterized my research efforts in the 1980s. At the beginning of this decade, I broadened my inquiry from Calkins to the first generation of American women psychologists, who entered the field around the turn of the century. I collaborated on this project with Elizabeth Scarborough, another psychologist with training and interest in the history of psychology. The research focus also shifted away from discovering women psychologists and their contributions. This is reflected in the text of a talk that I gave at the Fifth Berkshire Conference on the history of women, held at Vassar College in June, 1981. There I outlined work in progress, in collaboration with Elizabeth Scarborough, describing it as an attempt to reconstruct the lives and experiences of the first generation of women psychologists in the Unites States, paying attention to a set of problems that they faced as women seeking higher education and employment in a newly emerging discipline. The emphasis in that 1981 talk was no longer on specific individual women and their contributions, but rather on the shared experience of a generation of women.

As this shift of emphasis was occurring in my historical research, I started teaching a seminar in history that concentrated on women psychologists. After offering the seminar for three consecutive years, I described my approach and the outcome in an article published in *Teaching of Psychology* (Furumoto, 1985). I began by expressing my surprise that nowhere in the many articles on the history course published in the pages of *Teaching of Psychology* in the previous decade had anyone voiced concern over the fact that typically women psychologists are made invisible in such courses. As the course is traditionally taught, I maintained, students come away believing that women have played little or no role in the discipline, whereas, in fact, women's participation and contribution to the discipline in the United States goes back almost 100 years. Noting that absence or invisibility of women is not unique to the history of psychology, I observed that it has, until quite recently, been true of historical accounts in general. I went on to discuss the relatively new field of women's history and its implications for teaching the history of psychology.

Women's History

Spurred by the women's movement of the late 1960s, a body of scholarship has grown up in the past twenty years that is called "women's history." American historian Gerda Lerner, a central figure in this field, has articulated a model for understanding the enterprise that has relevance for the history of psychology. She presented her model in a collection of essays (Lerner, 1979), written in the 1970s, in which she explains her views on women's history, why it is important, and how it differs from standard history.

Lerner observed that women, who represent half of human experience, have been largely excluded from history. In fact, she maintained that history, as traditionally written, can properly be thought of as the "history of men." What are her recommendations for beginning to place women in history? Lerner sees a starting point in what she calls "compensatory history," an approach in which the historian searches the past to find lost or overlooked women and uses them to fill up the empty niches in traditional history. Other names that have been applied to this brand of scholarship are the "history of women worthies" and the "add-women-and-stir approach." The next stage of women's history proposed by Lerner is what she terms "contribution history." Here, it is a movement which is of primary concern (e.g., the Progressive movement), and women are important or of interest only in terms of their contributions to that movement—contributions evaluated according to standards set by men.

Compensatory and contribution history do answer the questions "Who were the women in history?" and "What did they contribute?" and Lerner acknowledges them as necessary first steps. Yet, in her view, they do not in themselves provide an adequate women's history. She sees part of their deficiency rooted in the fact that most history has been written by men, and a history of women as written by men has "a special character, a built-in distortion: it comes to us refracted through the lens of men's observations; refracted again through values which consider man the measure" (p. 160). Arguing that women's "culturally determined and psychologically internalized marginality . . . makes their historical experience essentially different from men" (p. xxxi), Lerner describes the past as gendered. Therefore, in order to tap women's experience, the scholar must "ask what would history be like if it were seen through the eyes of women and ordered by values they define?" (p. 178).

What is the relevance of Lerner's analysis for teaching the history of psychology? It suggests that although placing women in the traditional course may very well begin with the rediscovery of lost women and their contributions to the discipline, it should not end there. An adequate history of women in the discipline needs to reconstruct the experience of those women as they lived their lives and as they worked to establish their professional identities. This approach to including women in the history of psychology course does not dismiss or deny the importance of history of ideas and systems in psychology or the life histories of the men in the discipline. It does maintain that even when all of those have been taken into consideration, something remains missing from the account. That something is the women's story: who they were, what they contributed, and what their experience was.

How does Lerner's model and, more generally, women's history relate to the new history outlined in the first part of this chapter? Women's history is typically viewed as one variety of the new history (Himmelfarb, 1987; Norton, 1986), presenting a challenge to the traditional approach which with its concentration on politics, economics, and diplomacy virtually excludes women from historical consideration. Within women's history itself, one is confronted with myriad points of view (Berkin & Norton, 1979; Cott & Pleck, 1979; Kerber, 1988; Scott, 1983). Lerner's model encompasses three of these, two of which—compensatory and contribution—have, aside from their focus on women, much in common with the old history of men. The other, which asserts that the past is gendered or, in other words, that the experience of men and women is and has been so different that each requires its own historical account, is a more radical departure from traditional history.

While not denying the importance of gender-specific experience, there are women's historians who, uneasy with the separation and even isolation of women that this approach fosters, have recently been charting other courses for their scholarship. Some are seeking to understand gender as a "socially constructed category of behavior that affects both sexes," while others, seeing pitfalls in an exclusive preoccupation with "women and their own perceptions of themselves and their struggles," are trying to situate women's experience within the broader political or economic context (Norton, 1986, p. 41).

Seminar on Early Women Psychologists

To give history of psychology instructors a concrete example of how women might be incorporated into the course, my *Teaching of Psychology* article (Furumoto, 1985) also contained a description of a seminar I had taught. The students were women undergraduates, most of whom were psychology majors planning careers in psychology or related fields. As I have already indicated, the focus of the seminar was my own research interest, women in the history of American psychology.

At the beginning of the term, I asked my students to choose a woman psychologist from the group of over 50 that appear in the first three editions of *American Men of Science* (Cattell, 1906; Cattell, 1910; and Cattell & Brimhall, 1921). Each then carried out research on her psychologist that formed the basis for writing a biographical essay. In the second half of the term, prior to writing the essay, each student reported to the seminar on the progress she was making in reconstructing the life of her psychologist. In the biographical essay, I asked for a description of the origins, educational experience, and career pattern of the woman psychologist studied. The students were also to discuss the school or system with which the woman psychologist was associated and to situate her in a historical context that reached beyond the discipline of psychology.

Students in the seminar read a standard history of psychology textbook, supplemented by selected papers on historiography of psychology and topics in the history of psychology, as well as by lectures, slides, films, class discussions, and short writing assignments. Throughout the term I tried to integrate learning about the history of psychology with reading, lectures, and discussion on women's history and the history of women in psychology. We dealt primarily with the period from 1890 to 1920, when American psychology was emerging and becoming established as a discipline and a profession.

My goal, in taking this approach, was to involve students in the experience of one woman psychologist and in the concrete details of that individual's life. They were asked to document that life as extensively as possible, and then to try to view it in the context of what was happening in American psychology in the late nineteenth and early twentieth centuries. Finally, students were instructed to relate their psychologist's life to what they had learned about the life experiences of American women from similar class and ethnic backgrounds during the same historical period.

In most respects the seminar was rewarding to students and instructor, and over the three years I taught it, student evaluations were quite positive. Many students remarked that the seminar was significant to them in that for the first time they became aware of the substantial number of women in the history of American psychology. Further, they came to appreciate the circumstances of these women's lives and to see how they contributed to the early development of the discipline. Some students commented that they found the seminar to be a new kind of learning experience in which individual projects and collective group work were closely integrated.

While the seminar was successful overall, it was not without problems. Some students became frustrated in their search for archival materials and information on their women psychologists, and at least one questioned whether it was worth the effort. Others had difficulty developing a historical perspective on the material. Some students were dismayed when, in the course of their research, they discovered the many compromises that these early psychologists were compelled to make. For example, they encountered some women who had been derailed from their careers because they chose to marry and others who managed to forge careers, only to be perceived as deviant and sometimes as social isolates. Few of the women psychologists, if any, managed to have it all.

Two students wrote an account of the seminar that appeared in the Undergraduate Update section of the APA *Monitor.* The article, by Natalie Golden and Christina Van Horn (1984), Wellesley College Class of 1983, began: "Ten undergraduate students majoring in various fields encountered excitement, satisfaction and frustration when they entered the world of historical research . . . . We quickly learned that doing primary research meant that we had to become detectives, searching through a historical maze that often yielded its clues only reluctantly" (p. 31).

Golden and Van Horn also described the research process as it unfolded during the semester: "Our principal task was to obtain whatever primary source material was available for a biographical essay. . . . Our searches led us to archivists (some more cooperative than others), family members, small town officials, colleagues and friends of the person we came to think of as 'my psychologist,' and in two cases, to the actual psychologist. Despite the differences among the psychologists, our discussions revealed many similar themes in the private and professional lives of these women." Summarizing the seminar, they characterized it as "a shared quest that gave each of us recognition and the entire group satisfaction and stimulation" (p. 31).

Beyond Compensatory and Contribution History

Teaching the seminar and writing an article on it resulted in an unanticipated fringe benefit. Namely, it helped me clarify my thinking about the nature and direction of my research in history. Returning to Lerner's (1979) model of women's history, it was clear that in my study of Mary Calkins I had begun with compensatory and contribution history. Although this approach is different from traditional history in the sense that it is concerned with a woman rather than a man, I concur with Lerner's assessment that it does not represent a serious challenge to traditional history.

In the early 1980s, persuaded by Lerner's arguments regarding the necessity to move beyond compensatory and contribution history, I began to attempt the reconstruction of women's experience. This was to become a central focus of the work completed by Elizabeth Scarborough and myself in subsequent years—work that resulted, in part, in an article (Furumoto & Scarborough, 1986) in the *American Psychologist* and a book (Scarborough & Furumoto, 1987), both concerned with the first generation of American women psychologists. This recent work reflects increased sensitivity to the major dimensions of the new history that I mentioned previously. Specifically, in contrast with traditional history, it is more contextual, more critical, more inclusive, more archival, and more past-minded. To illustrate concretely these differences between the new and the old history, I will offer you an example from my own work, contrasting my earlier more traditional scholarship with my later work that reflects the influence of the new history.

Perusing my earlier work on Calkins, you will find a traditional biographical account; the following is a sample of that genre:

> Mary Calkins was born in 1863, the eldest of five children, and grew up in Buffalo, New York, where her father was a Protestant minister. In 1881, the family moved to Newton, Massachusetts, a city about 12 miles west of Boston, where The Reverend Wolcott Calkins had accepted the pastorate of a Congregational church. After completing high school in Newton, Mary Calkins went to Smith College, where she graduated in 1885.
>
> Shortly after completing her undergraduate study at Smith, Calkins accompanied her family to Europe, where they traveled for more than a year. Upon their return to New England in fall 1887, Calkins was offered a job teaching Greek at Wellesley College, a woman's college located just a few miles from her family home in Newton. She accepted the position and thus began a more than 40-year association with that institution, where she was to spend her entire career.
>
> After having been at Wellesley little over a year, Calkins' talent as a teacher and her interest in philosophy prompted a professor in the philosophy department to recommend to the college president that Calkins be appointed to a newly created position in experimental psychology. The appointment was made contingent upon Calkins' studying the subject for a year, an undertaking that required petitions and special arrangements since neither Clark University, where she was tutored by E. C. Sanford, nor Harvard, where she had attended the seminars of William James and Josiah Royce, was willing to admit women as students at that time. Upon her return to Wellesley in the autumn of 1891, Calkins established a psychological laboratory and introduced the new scientific psychology into the curriculum.

> A year later, feeling the need for additional study, Calkins returned to Harvard to work in the psychological laboratory of Hugo Münsterberg. There, pursuing research on factors influencing memory, she invented what has come to be known as the paired-associate technique. Although by the fall of 1894 she had completed all the requirements for the PhD and her Harvard professors enthusiastically recommended that it be awarded to her, the institutional authorities refused because she was a woman.
>
> Calkins, as mentioned earlier, spent her entire career at Wellesley College, teaching, developing a system of self-psychology, publishing prolifically in both psychology and philosophy, and achieving recognition in both fields. She was the first woman to be elected president of the American Psychological Association in 1905, and of the American Philosophical Association in 1918. Honorary degrees were bestowed on Calkins by Columbia University in 1909 and her alma mater, Smith, in 1910, and she was elected to honorary membership in the British Psychological Association in 1928.

This brief account of Calkins' life and career is characteristic of the approach I took in my early work and can be appropriately labeled compensatory and contribution history. In order to move beyond these initial forms of women's history to an inquiry that illuminates Calkins' experience requires adopting a stance that I have called "past-mindedness." It is similar to an approach labeled "historicism" (Stocking, 1965) originally articulated by Butterfield (1931/1959), a historian who argued in favor of "trying to understand the past for the sake of the past" rather than "studying the past for the sake of the present" (p. 16). That is, historical understanding should be sought by attempting to place oneself in the past and seeing things through the eyes of the actors at that time. The vehicle for achieving this perspective is serious and sustained immersion in published and unpublished documents of the time and in the relevant historical scholarship.

In the early 1980s, Elizabeth Scarborough and I took on this task for Calkins and the two dozen or so other women we called "the first generation of American women psychologists." It led us to archives large and small throughout the United States, from Berkeley to Columbia, from Akron to Chicago. It involved us with work of women's historians, educational historians, and historians of science. And eventually it paid off. We began to feel our way into the concrete reality of the early women psychologists' lives and to detect certain recurrent gender-specific themes that we took as a framework for the section of our book called "The Difference Being a Woman Made" (Scarborough & Furumoto, 1987). These themes were barriers to graduate education, the family claim, the marriage versus career dilemma, uncollegiality of male colleagues, and the myth of meritocracy.

In five separate chapters (one for each theme), we told the story of a woman psychologist whose life experience provided a vivid example of that theme. If we explore Calkins' life in terms of these themes, we have a markedly different account from the one yielded by compensatory and contribution history. Take, for example, the family claim and the marriage-versus-career dilemma. Our research unearthed convincing evidence, corroborated by other scholarship in women's history, that in the late nineteenth century, women, unlike men, were required to choose between pursuing an academic career and marriage. In our group about half the women eventually married, and it was clear that a woman who chose to marry in that era sabotaged her career in academic psychology, which at the time was just about all of psychology. We also became aware of a phenomenon that the founder of Hull House, Jane Addams, had termed "the family claim." The family claim referred to the fact that a middle-class daughter, and especially an unmarried one, had numerous obligations to her family members, and the responsibilities these entailed were expected to take precedence over her vocational interests and aspirations.

Both of these themes, the marriage-versus-career dilemma and the family claim, were salient features of Calkins' experience. Never married, she lived in her parents' home for her entire life, and as their sole surviving daughter, she, rather than her three brothers, took on increasing responsibility for her aging parents' welfare. In her notes for an address to a group of women students at Bryn Mawr College (1911), Calkins mused over the hardships of the life of the woman scholar, particularly those of not being able to marry and have a family of her own and of having to bear heavy responsibility for her parents' care.

Speaking of adjustments necessitated by "the often conflicting claims of scholarship and life in its social relations," Calkins observed that while this adjustment is "seldom easy for anyone," it "is particularly difficult in the lives of most women." In support of this claim, she pointed to the acceptance of the view "that a woman has more exacting social and especially family obligations than a man." Maintaining that these norms affected not only "the woman who is a mother" but the unmarried woman as well, Calkins noted "the chances are, for example, that the unmarried daughter rather than the unmarried son, if a choice becomes necessary, should undertake the responsibility for their parents' home."

I have tried to illustrate by this discussion of gender-specific themes in relation to Calkins that in reconstructing the experience of actors in the past, we reveal dimensions of their lives undisclosed by a more traditional approach to history. Furthermore, being aware of these dimensions can sometimes help us understand why their careers as psychologists assumed the particular shapes they did. For example, realizing the potency of the family claim makes intelligible Calkins' decision to decline a joint Columbia-Barnard professorship offered by James McKeen Cattell in 1905.

As she wrote to her mentor Hugo Müsterberg, in part she had reservations about the kind of work the position might entail, but she also disclosed to him that she was held back by her sense of responsibility to her parents. Describing the position to Münsterberg, Calkins wrote, "I think that Barnard needs and desires someone to start a small undergraduate psychological laboratory, and that I have no wish to do. Nor did I see any good chance for me to do the work, on that faculty, which I am best fitted to do; for the field is already well occupied. This is my professional consolation for the decision with which, personally, I am well content. I think I shall teach subjects which better suit my capacity, and accordingly that I shall write more and better, at Wellesley than at Barnard-Columbia."

The personal consideration that Calkins told Münsterberg was the deciding factor had to do with her parents. "I was unwilling to leave my house, both because I find in it my deepest happiness and because I feel that I add to the happiness of my mother's and father's lives. They would have considered transferring the house to New York, but I became convinced that it would be distinctly hurtful to them to do so" (Calkins, 1905, June 18).

In a more candid letter written to her younger brother Raymond, Mary Calkins revealed that concern for the welfare of her ailing 74-year-old father precluded her from even seriously considering the job in New York City. As Calkins explained to her brother, "I have decided as you thought I would not to go to New York. The deciding factor was my certainty that father ought to stay here. To be sure on this point, I consulted Dr. Blake who said that father ought not to have the nervous strain accompanying a complete readjustment of his life. This settled the matter beyond hesitation. I am not sure how I should have decided without this" (Calkins, 1905, June 8).

Sometimes a richly detailed reconstruction of past experience may even provide insight into the source of a psychologist's theoretical orientation not available through other means. This is precisely what happened to me recently as, in the process of writing an address on Calkins, I pondered a question that has puzzled me for many years: Why was Calkins so firmly committed to self-psychology in an era of militant behaviorism? What now seems to me to be a very plausible answer lies in the particular institutional context of Wellesley College in the late 19th and early 20th centuries, when Calkins was formulating her system of self-psychology.

Educational historian Patricia A. Palmieri (1983), who has recently completed a study of the early faculty at Wellesley, found an atmosphere there dramatically different from that existing in male-dominated institutions of the day. Wellesley, with its all-female, all-single professoriate, formed a close-knit women's community in which deeply felt and long-lasting relationships flourished. Palmieri characterized the group of 53 academic women who formed the basis of her study as "strikingly homogeneous in terms of social and geographic origins, upbringing, and sociocultural world-view" (p. 197).

Explaining what life was like in this community of academic women who had so much in common, Palmieri described it as "very much like an extended family. Its members, with shared backgrounds and tastes, shared visions of life and work, and often shared bonds of family or prior friendship, could hardly but produce an extraordinary community. In this milieu, no one was isolated, no one forgotten" (p. 203). Palmieri observes that in contrast to our contemporary society where "occupational and private selves rarely meet, the academic women of Wellesley conjoined public and private spheres" and became "not merely professional associates but astoundingly good friends" (p. 203).

Wellesley's institutional context stands in marked contrast to the university settings where most male psychologists were developing their theories and carrying out their research. Of Johns Hopkins in that same period, historian Hugh Hawkins (1960) noted the unbreachable gulf that existed between isolated specialized researchers, and how extremely difficult the men found it to get to know fellow faculty. One senior professor at Johns Hopkins pictured the situation thus: "we only get glimpses of what is going forward in the minds and hearts of our colleagues. We are like trains moving on parallel tracks. We catch sight of some face, some form that appeals to us and it is gone" (p. 237).

Returning to the question of why Mary Calkins became so intensely committed to conceiving the subject matter of psychology as the self, and more specifically interacting social selves, in the heyday of behaviorism, once one appreciates the Wellesley context of her era, the answer seems almost embarrassingly obvious. From the time she entered the Wellesley community in 1887 until her death in 1930, her personal and professional lives were closely intertwined with those of Her Wellesley friends and colleagues. Although trained in the mainstream academic, laboratory psychology of the 1890s by her male professors at Harvard and Clark, she soon thereafter came to question the atomistic, impersonal conception of the subject matter characteristic of this approach, and still later, she rejected it outright.

As Edna Heidbreder put it in a paper on the topic of Calkins' self psychology, Calkins came to see "the classical experimental psychologists as out of touch . . . with important portions of . . . [the] subject matter [of psychology] as it presents itself in ordinary experience as she herself observed it and as she believed, by checking with others, that they too observed it" (Heidbreder, 1972, p. 63). It is worth noting here that the classical experimental psychologists referred to were for the most part male psychologists, in university environments, whose experience as isolated specialists was vastly different from that of Calkins. It is not surprising then that the alternative to the classical experimental view espoused by Calkins concerned itself with something of the utmost significance to her and to the other women with whom she shared her Wellesley world, namely the reality and importance of selves in everyday experience.

Conclusion

I have tried to convey to you in this chapter how the new history of psychology differs from the old and to describe some ways in which the new history can enhance our understanding of the past. In conclusion, I want to consider briefly the implications of the new history for teaching the history of psychology.

First and foremost, the new history alerts us to the need to move beyond traditional textbook history of psychology. Much has been written about the problematic nature of textbook history in science, in general, as well as in psychology, in particular. In his classic work, *The Structure of Scientific Revolutions,* Thomas Kuhn (1970) observed that textbooks in science and the historical tradition they supply are rewritten after every scientific revolution. In these texts, Kuhn says, "partly by selection and partly by distortion, the scientists of earlier ages are implicitly represented as having worked on the same set of fixed problems, and in accordance with the same set of fixed canons that the most recent revolution in scientific theory and method has made seem scientific" (p. 138). What is accomplished by the portrayal of a discipline's past as developing linearly and cumulatively toward its present vantage, according to Kuhn, is that "both students and professionals come to feel like participants in a long-standing historical tradition" (p. 138). However, Kuhn warns, this rewriting of history backward from the present also serves to truncate scientists' sense of their discipline's history.

Kuhn's view (1968) in regard to textbook history of science in general has been voiced in the 1980s with respect to textbook history of psychology in particular. Historian of science Mitchell G. Ash (1983) has advanced the claim that a particularly important function of the history of psychology as practiced in the United States has been what he calls "pedagogical self-presentation." That is, textbook history aimed at beginning and advanced students that portrays psychology as a science and as descended from an ancient tradition of knowledge has served the discipline as a legitimation strategy. Ash distinguishes between such textbook history and historical scholarship in psychology, noting that the recent scholarship is currently yielding results that may not be compatible with textbook versions of psychology's past. The recent scholarship that Ash refers to is what I have described as the new history of psychology, and I concur with his assertion that this work poses a challenge to much of what appears in textbook accounts. Given this state of affairs, what is the teacher of the history course to do?

My recommendation is that we move beyond textbook history into the new history of psychology posthaste. This will mean teaching a history that is more contextual, more critical, more archival, more inclusive, and more past-minded. Above all, it will require a change in emphasis from the way in which we psychologists have traditionally approached the history of our discipline. This change involves a shift from focusing on great men and their ideas to reconstructing particular sociohistorical contexts.

Charles Rosenberg (1987) described these differing emphases succinctly in a recent editorial in the history of science journal *Isis* that commented on the history, current status, and future of that field as the journal approached its 75th anniversary. In the early years of the journal, Rosenberg noted, work in the history of science was carried on by scientists and scholars who were practitioners of other disciplines. In contrast, most of the work currently published in *Isis* is by professional historians of science.

Those past generations of historians who were practitioners of other disciplines often neglected what, in Rosenberg's view, is a fundamental aspect of the current historian's task. He urges contemporary historians of science not to be guilty of the same oversight. I believe that his words of advice to historians are also an appropriate exhortation to teachers of the history of psychology, and I offer them to you in conclusion: "We must strive to understand the richness and relatedness of past experience. The scientist has been an actor in specific historical settings, not simply a solver of cognitive dilemmas" (p. 517).

References

Allport, G. (1968). The historical background of modern social psychology. In G. Lindzey & E. Aronson (Eds.), *The handbook of social psychology, Vol. 1* (2nd ed.), (pp. 1-80). Reading, MA: Addison Wesley.

Ash, M. G. (1983). The self-presentation of a discipline: History of psychology in the United States between pedagogy and scholarship. In L. Graham, W. Lepenies, & P. Weingart (Eds.), *Functions and uses of disciplinary histories, Vol. 7* (pp. 143-189). Dordrecht, Holland: D. Reidel.

Ash, M. G., & Woodward, W. R. (Eds.). (1987). *Psychology in twentieth-century thought and society.* New York: Cambridge University Press.

Benjamin, L. T., Jr. (Ed.). (1988). *A history of psychology: Original sources and contemporary research.* New York: McGraw-Hill.
Berkin, C. R., & Norton, M. B. (Eds.). (1979). *Women of America: A history.* Boston: Houghton Mifflin.
Bernstein, M. D., & Russo, N. F. (1974). The history of psychology revisited, or up with our foremothers. *American Psychologist, 29,* 130-134.
Blumenthal, A. L. (1975), A reappraisal of Wilhelm Wundt. *American Psychologist, 30,* 1081-1086.
Blumenthal, A. L. (1980). Wilhelm Wundt and early American psychology: A clash of cultures. In R. W. Rieber (Ed.), *Wilhelm Wundt and the making of a scientific psychology* (pp. 117-135). New York: Plenum.
Boring, E. G. (1929). *A history of experimental psychology.* New York: The Century Co.
Boring, E. G. (1950). *A history of experimental psychology* (2nd ed.). New York: Appleton-Century-Crofts.
Brush, S. G. (1974). Should the history of science be rated X? *Science, 183,* 1164-1172.
Burnham, J. C. (1988). *Paths into American culture: Psychology, medicine, and morals.* Philadelphia: Temple University Press.
Burt, C. (1966). The genetic determination of differences in intelligence. *British Journal of Psychology, 57,* 137-153.
Buss, A. R. (Ed.). (1979). *Psychology in social context.* New York: Irvington.
Butterfield, H. (1959). *The Whig interpretation of history.* London: G. Bell and Sons. (Orginial work published 1931.)
Calkins, M. W. (1905, June 8). Letter to R. Calkins. (From papers held by the Calkins family).
Calkins, M. W. (1905, June 18). Letter to H. Münsterberg. (From the Hugo Münsterberg Papers, Boston Public Library, Boston, MA).
Calkins, M. W. (1911). Notes for "The place of scholarship in life." (From the Wellesley College Archives, Wellesley, MA).
Capshew, J. H., & Lazlo, A. C. (1986). "We would not take no for an answer": Women psychologists and gender politics during World War II. *Journal of Social Issues, 42,* 157-180.
Cattell, J. McK. (Ed.). (1906). *American men of science.* New York: The Science Press.
Cattell, J. McK. (Ed.). (1910). *American men of science* (2nd ed.). New York: The Science Press.
Cattell, J. McK., & Brimhall, D. R. (Eds.). (1921). *American men of science* (3rd ed.). Garrison, NY: The Science Press.
Church, R. M. (1980). The Albert study: Illustration vs. evidence. *American Psychologist, 35,* 215-216.
Cornwell, D., Hobbs, S., & Prytula, R. (1980). Little Albert rides again. *American Psychologist, 35,* 216-217.
Cott, N. F., & Pleck, E. H. (Eds.). (1979). *A heritage of her own: Toward a new social history of American women.* New York: Simon and Schuster.
Danziger,K. (1979). The positivist repudiation of Wundt. *Journal of the History of the Behavioral Sciences, 15,* 205-230.
Danziger, K. (1980). Wundt and the two traditions of psychology. In R. W. Rieber (Ed.), *Wilhelm Wundt and the making of a scientific psychology* (pp. 73-87). New York: Plenum.

Danziger, K. (1985). The origins of the psychological experiment as a social institution. *American Psychologist, 40,* 133-140.
Finison, L. J. (1976). Unemployment, politics, and the history of organized psychology. *American Psychologist, 31,* 747-755.
Finison, L. J. (1978). Unemployment, politics, and the history of organized psychology, II: The Psychologists League, the WPA, and the National Health Program. *American Psychologist, 33,* 471-477.
Finison, L. J. (1986). The psychological insurgency, 1936-1945. *Journal of Social Issues, 42,* 21-35.
Furumoto, L. (1979). Mary Whiton Calkins (1863-1930): Fourteenth president of the American Psychological Association. *Journal of the History of the Behavioral Sciences, 15,* 346-356.
Furumoto, L. (1981, June). *First generation of U.S. women in psychology.* Paper presented at the Fifth Berkshire Conference on the History of Women, Vassar College, Poughkeepsie, NY.
Furumoto, L. (1985). Placing women in the history of psychology. *Teaching of Psychology, 12,* 203-206.
Furumoto, L., & Scarborough, E. (1986). Placing women in the history of psychology: The first American women psychologists. *American Psychologist, 41,* 35-42.
Golden, N., & Van Horn, C. (1984, February). Seminar focuses on early women leaders. *APA Monitor,* p. 31.
Guthrie, R. V. (1976). *Even the rat was white: A historical view of psychology.* New York: Harper & Row.
Harris, B. (1979). Whatever happened to little Albert? *American Psychologist, 34,* 151-160.
Harris, B. (1980). Ceremonial versus critical history of psychology. *American Psychologist, 35,* 218-219.
Harris, B., Unger, R. K., & Stagner, R. (Eds.). (1986). 50 years of psychology and social issues. *Journal of Social Issues, 42*(1).
Hawkins, H. (1960). *Pioneer: A history of the Johns Hopkins University, 1874-1889.* Ithaca, NY: Cornell University Press.
Hearnshaw, L. S. (1981). *Cyril Burt: Psychologist.* New York: Vintage Books. (Originally published by Cornell University Press, 1979).
Heidbreder, E. (1972). Mary Whiton Calkins: A discussion. *Journal of the History of the Behavior Sciences, 8,* 56-68.
Hilgard, E. R. (1987). *Psychology in America: A historical survey.* San Diego: Harcourt Brace Jovanovich.
Himmelfarb, G. (1987). *The new history and the old.* Cambridge, MA: Harvard University Press.
Kerber, L. K. (1988). Separate spheres, female worlds, woman's place: The rhetoric of women's history. *The Journal of American History, 75,* 9-39.
Kuhn, T. S. (1968). The history of science. In D. L. Sills (Ed.), *International Encyclopedia of the Social Sciences, Vol. 14* (pp. 74-83).
Kuhn, T. S. (1970). *The structure of scientific revolutions* (2nd ed.). Chicago: University of Chicago Press.
Leahey, T. H. (1981). The mistaken mirror: On Wundt's and Titchener's psychologies. *Journal of the History of the Behavioral Sciences, 17,* 273-282.
Leahey, T. H. (1987). *A history of psychology: Main currents in psychological thought* (2nd ed.). Englewood Cliffs, NJ: Prentice-Hall.

Leary, D. E. (1987). Telling likely stories: The rhetoric of the new psychology, 1880-1920. *Journal of the History of the Behavioral Sciences, 23,* 315-331.

Leary, D. E., & Koch, S. (Eds.). (1985). *A century of psychology as science.* New York: McGraw-Hill.

Lerner, G. (1979). *The majority finds its past: Placing women in history.* New York: Oxford University Press.

Morawski, J. G. (1986). Organizing knowledge and behavior at Yale's Institute of Human Relations. *Isis, 77,* 219-242.

Morawski, J. G. (Ed.). (1988). *The rise of experimentation in American psychology.* New Haven: Yale University Press.

Murray, F. S. (1980). Search for Albert. *American Psychologist, 35,* 217.

Napoli, D. S. (1981). *Architects of adjustment: The history of the psychological profession in the United States.* Port Washington, NY: Kennikat Press.

Norton, M. B. (1986, April 13). Is Clio a feminist? The new history. *New York Times,* pp. 1, 40-41.

O'Donnell, J. M. (1979). The crisis of experimentalism in the 1920s: E. G. Boring and his uses of history. *American Psychologist, 34,* 289-295.

O'Donnell, J. M. (1985). *The origins of behaviorism: American Psychology, 1870-1920.* New York: New York University Press.

Palmieri, P. A. (1983). Here was fellowship: A social portrait of academic women at Wellesley College, 1895-1920. *History of Education Quarterly, 23,* 195-214.

Pauly, P. J. (1986). G. Stanley Hall and his successors: A history of the first half century of psychology at Johns Hopkins. In S. H. Hulse & B. F. Green, Jr. (Eds.), *One hundred years of psychological research in America: G. Stanley Hall and the Johns Hopkins tradition* (pp. 21-51). Baltimore: Johns Hopkins University Press.

Robinson, J. H. (1912). *The new history.* New York: Macmillan.

Rosenberg, C. (1987). *Isis* at seventy-five [Editorial]. *Isis, 78,* 515-517.

Samelson, F. (1974). History, origin myth and ideology: "Discovery" of social psychology. *Journal for the Theory of Social Behaviour, 4,* 217-231.

Samelson, F. (1980). J. B. Watson's little Albert, Cyril Burt's twins, and the need for a critical science. *American Psychologist, 35,* 619-625.

Samelson, F. (1985). Organizing for the kingdom of behavior: Academic battles and organizational policies in the twenties. *Journal of the History of the Behavioral Sciences, 21,* 33-47.

Scarborough, E., & Furumoto, L. (1987). *Untold lives: The first generation of American women psychologists.* New York: Columbia University Press.

Scott, J. W. (1983). Women in history: The modern period. *Past and Present, 101,* 141-157.

Seligman, M. E. P. (1980). Harris on selective misrepresentation: A selective misrepresentation of Seligman. *American Psychologist, 35,* 214-215.

Sokal, M. M. (Ed.). (1987). *Psychological testing and American society, 1890-1930.* New Brunswick, NJ: Rutgers University Press.

Stocking, G. W., Jr. (1965). On the limits of "presentism" and "historicism" in the historiography of the behavioral sciences [Editorial]. *Journal of the History of the Behavioral Sciences, 1,* 211-218.

Tweney, R. D., & Yachanin, S. A. (1980). Titchener's Wundt. In W. G. Bringmann & R. D. Tweney (Eds.), *Wundt studies: A centennial collection* (pp. 380-395). Toronto: C. J. Hogrefe.

Walsh, M. R. (1985). Academic professional women organizing for change: The struggle in psychology. *Journal of Social Issues, 41,* 17-27.
Watson, J. B., & Rayner, R. (1920). Conditioned emotional reactions. *Journal of Experimental Psychology, 3,* 1-14.
Watson, R. I. (1975). The history of psychology as a specialty: A personal view of its first 15 years. *Journal of the History of the Behavioral Sciences, 11,* 5-14.
Woodward, W. R. (1980). Toward a critical historiography of psychology. In J. Brozek & L. J. Pongratz (Eds.). *Historiography of modern psychology* (pp. 29-67). Toronto: Hogrefe.
Woodward, W. R., & Ash, M. G. (Eds.). (1982). *The problematic science: Psychology in nineteenth-century thought.* New York: Praeger.
Young, R. M. (1966). Scholarship and the history of the behavioural sciences. *History of Science, 5,* 1-51.

CARROLL E. IZARD

THE STRUCTURE AND FUNCTIONS OF EMOTIONS: IMPLICATIONS FOR COGNITION, MOTIVATION, AND PERSONALITY

Carroll E. Izard received his BA degree from Mississippi College and a BD from Yale University Divinity School. He received his PhD degree in clinical psychology from Syracuse University.

Izard is Unidel Professor of Psychology at the University of Delaware. He has written or edited 12 books, including *The Face of Emotion,* winner of the 1969 Elliot Memorial Award; 40 book chapters; and about 100 journal articles and technical reports. His recent work includes the chapter on emotions in the recent revision of *Stevens' Handbook of Experimental Psychology* and the article on emotions for the 1990 *Encyclopaedia Britannica.* In 1985–86 he served on the National Research Council's workgroup on emotion and motivation, and he has been a consulting editor for *Psychological Review, Journal of Personality and Social Psychology, Motivation and Emotion,* and other journals. He is a Fellow of the American Association for the Advancement of Science and the American Psychological Association's Personality and Social, Clinical, and Consulting Divisions.

Izard has been influenced by the works of Charles Darwin, William James, John Dollard, Chester Bliss, and Silvan Tomkins. He now focuses on early emotional development, with an emphasis on emotion regulation and the relations of emotions to temperament, personality, and social competence.

CARROLL E. IZARD

THE STRUCTURE AND FUNCTIONS OF EMOTIONS: IMPLICATIONS FOR COGNITION, MOTIVATION, AND PERSONALITY

There are more than a dozen approaches to the study of emotions. They can be roughly classified into two broad categories: biosocial and cognitive-social, or constructivist. This grouping is an oversimplification, but it should help us get a handle on what may be the most rapidly growing area of psychology.

Many of the differences between these two categories of theory stem from differing assumptions regarding the role of genes and biological processes in emotions. Biosocial theories assume that important features of emotions are rooted in our biological makeup and that the genes we inherit are significant determinants of the threshold and characteristic intensity level of each basic emotion. In this view, our emotional life is a function of the interaction of genetic tendencies and the evaluative system, beliefs, and roles we acquire through experience. On the other hand, cognitive-social theories assume that genetic factors are inconsequential and that emotions are cognitively constructed, deriving strictly from interactions of the person with the environment, particularly the social environment. Accordingly, our emotions are a function of our appraisals of the world around us, the culture in which we live, and what we learn.

This work was supported in part by NSF Grant No. BNS8706146 and NIMH Grant No. MH4205003.

I have relied on biosocial theory and research throughout this paper, and based it on the principle that human development and human behaviors are a result of interactions or transactions among genes, culture, and individual-specific experiences. I am also guided by the equally important complementary principle that emotions exert highly significant organizing and motivational influences on developmental processes, cognition, and action. Although my approach is biosocial, I shall identify some of the issues where there is major theoretical controversy and provide references for the contrasting views and research of cognitive-social theorists. I shall also note some important agreements. Fortunately, in some cases, research inspired by one approach—for example, studies of the influence of cognitively-induced emotion on memory and behavior—can be interpreted by both biosocial theorists and constructivists as supportive of their views. This is a promising development, but we are still far from a unified theory of emotions.

In this paper I will be discussing five interrelated topics or issues: (a) emotion activation; (b) the structure of emotions; (c) the functions of emotion; (d) emotions, motivation, and adaptation; and (e) emotions, temperament, and personality. How do they influence our perception, thought, memory, and action? Are emotions of major significance in human motivation? What are the processes involved in the control or regulation of emotions? Is there any stability in the way an individual responds emotionally? How do emotions relate to temperament and personality?

Before discussing these current issues in the field of emotions, one historical issue should be reviewed briefly. Almost 50 years ago, some theorists proposed that concepts of separate and distinct emotions like joy and sadness could not be fruitfully studied by scientific method (Duffy, 1941). They suggested that all emotion-related phenomena could be explained in terms of global, undifferential arousal and that differences in emotion states were simply differences in levels of the intensity of such arousal. In this context, arousal referred to activity in the brain and nervous system brought about by stimulation of the ascending reticular activating system, a neural mechanism located in the brain stem. In the framework of arousal or activation theory, one could speak of emotion as an entity.

Arousal as a unitary dimension for explaining emotion is no longer a viable concept and the idea of a number of distinct emotions is now widely accepted by biosocial and cognitive theorists. In the years since the introduction of arousal theory, scientific methods have been developed for the study of discrete emotions, and research has yielded evidence of several different types of arousal (Dienstbier, in press; Gray, 1982). A few studies have produced data showing that each of several specific emotions is accompanied by a distinct pattern of neural activity in the somatic or autonomic nervous system (Ax,

1953; Ekman, Levenson, & Friesen, 1983; Rusalova, Izard, & Simonov, 1975; Schwartz, 1982).

This historical issue was briefly reviewed here in order to emphasize that emotions can be studied scientifically and that significant progress has been made in the understanding of emotional phenomena. It also demonstrates that it is no longer appropriate to speak or write of *emotion* in the singular form unless one is referring to one specific emotion or making a point about emotion in relation to another type of process such as cognition or action. It is appropriate to speak of *emotions* in the plural form, signifying the existence of several distinct emotions like joy and sadness, anger and fear. Arousal theorists were correct in believing that emotions have a neurophysiological component, but they contributed little to our knowledge of how neural processes are transformed into emotion expressions and emotion experiences.

The Structures and Processes of Emotion Activation

What causes an emotion? What structures and processes are involved? The question as to precisely how an emotion is triggered has been one of the most captivating and controversial topics in the field of emotions. To address the question properly, it needs to be broken down, made more precise. Emotions involve neural processes, bodily changes, and mental activity, and the following discussion of emotion activation will consider each of these three types of processes.

It is easy for us to think of things that make us happy or sad, but it is not yet possible for anyone to explain precisely how the feeling of joy or sadness occurs. Neuroscience has produced far more information about the processes leading to the physiological responses and expressive behavior of emotion than about those that generate the conscious experience of emotion. In a later section, I shall summarize the main ideas that scientists have used to explain this process.

Neural Processes in Emotion Activation

An emotion can be activated by events occurring within the individual or by a combination of internal and external events and processes. Emotion activation by internal events might begin in the young infant with hunger. The drive state intensifies, hunger pangs become painful, and the pain activates anger. Studies have shown that pain can produce anger in the 2-month-old infant, who is too young to appraise, categorize, or interpret the agent of harm (Izard, Hembree, Dougherty, & Spizzirri, 1983). In such cases, the data leading to the emotion are processed in innate neural circuits that evolved as characteristics of the species.

The findings of neuroscience indicate that stimuli are evaluated for emotional significance when information from primary receptors (in the visual, tactual, auditory, or other sensory systems) travels along certain neural pathways to the limbic forebrain. Stimuli processed in this way are coded for their emotion-eliciting value. Although there is no reason to believe that we cannot discover the pathways for processing information relating to each of the basic emotions, most empirical data relate to the pathways for processing information that elicit anger and fear.

LeDoux (1987) and his coworkers described the circuits involved in the processing of acoustic stimuli that lead to fear in the rat. Their data show that auditory fear conditioning involves the transmission of sound signals through the auditory pathway to the thalamus (medial geniculate body) and thence to the dorsal amygdala.

LeDoux hypothesized that emotion activated by way of the thalamoamygdala pathways results from rapid, minimal, automatic, evaluative processing. Such processing probably results only in the detection of certain sensory characteristics and little or no perceptual organization. Emotion activated in this way need not involve the neocortex. Emotion activated by discrimination of stimulus features, organized perceptions, thoughts, or memories requires that the information be relayed from the thalamus to the amygdala and neocortex. Such a circuit is thought to be the neural basis for cognitive appraisal and evaluation of events. Thus there are two circuits for evaluating stimuli for emotion information, one subcortical and one involving the neocortex (see Figure 1). Apparently, there is sufficient independence between the thalamoamygdala and thalamocortical pathways that the former can activate emotion without involving the latter.

If we generalize from the rat brain to the human brain, then the two-circuit model of the neural pathways in emotion activation has several important theoretical implications. The evidence relating to the thalamoamygdala pathway is consistent with the evidence that prerepresentational infants of two months respond emotionally to pain (Izard, Hembree, & Huebner, 1987) and that adult subjects can develop preferences or make affective judgments about objects before they can demonstrate recognition memory for them (Zajonc, 1980). Such affective responses are apparently based on the detection and registration of minimal sensory characteristics and do not involve complete perceptual organization or cognitive appraisal. Actually, higher order cognitive-evaluative processes in the thalamoamygdala pathway are not possible because it is a subcortical circuit. Thus we can respond emotionally to certain events before we have sufficient cognitive capacity or sufficient time for evaluation and perceptual or-

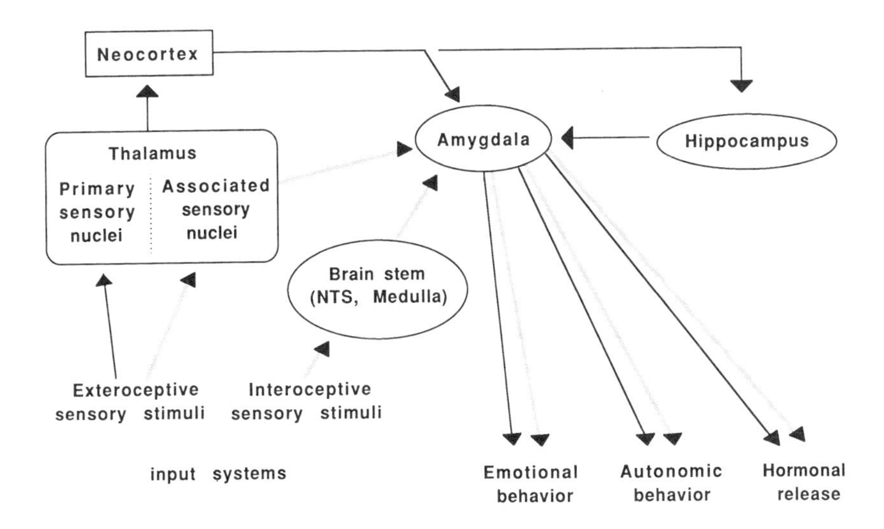

Figure 1. Subcortical ——▸ and corticolimbic ——▸ pathways in emotion activation. Adapted from LeDoux (1987) with permission. Copyright 1987, American Physiological Society.

ganization. When confronted with a complex event that engages the neocortex and requires processing in the corticoamygdala pathway, the initial emotion stemming from subcortical processes may influence the higher order appraisal processes.

In very early human development, we might expect that most emotion expressions derive from subcortical processing, with minimal cortical involvement. As cognitive capacities increase with maturation and learning, the neocortex and corticoamygdala pathway (or other corticolimbic pathways) become more and more involved. By the time children acquire language and the capacity for long-term memory, they probably process most events in both subcortical and corticolimbic pathways. The neural-evaluative pathways probably go to work simultaneously (parallel processing), with the subcortical pathway providing the rapid, primitive data and initial emotion response and the corticolimbic pathway providing the precise information for perceptual organization, discrimination, comparison, appraisal, categorization, and the adjusted emotion response.

Physiological Processes in Emotion Activation

Many theorists agree that feedback from bodily or physiological activity contributes to emotion activation. There is disagreement as to what kind of feedback is important. Some think that it is visceral feedback or feedback from the activity of the smooth-muscle organs innervated by the autonomic nervous system (ANS), such as the stomach and heart. Others think that it is feedback via the somatic nervous system or feedback from the voluntary, striated muscles, especially of the face.

Visceral feedback. When emotion first became a topic in science, theorists suggested that the sensations arising from expressive behavior and visceral responses constituted a critical link in the process leading to an emotion experience. Charles Darwin (1872/1965) believed that you could change your emotion experience by willfully changing your behavior—facial expression, posture, gesture. Smile, hold your head high, and walk with a sprightly gait in order to suppress sadness and experience joy. William James (1884) took this idea a step further, a step beyond common sense. He put it this way, using fear as an example. The perception of the threatening event sets your muscles in action, resulting in facial expression, increases in heart rate and respiration, and, perhaps rapid retreat. Then, your perception of these bodily changes constitute the feeling or subjective experience of fear. Thus, in the words made famous by James, We do not run because we are afraid. We are afraid because we run. There is little evidence to support this notion that feedback from the viscera determines the quality of emotion (Chwalisz, Diener, & Gallagher, 1988; LeDoux, 1986). However, modified versions of James' model of emotion activation are still debated in psychology.

Somatic feedback. The changes that have been made in James' position include changes in language. James' phrase for the critical causal process, *perception of bodily changes,* is now termed *transformed sensory feedback,* meaning somatic feedback, especially from muscles of the face. Thus some current biosocial theorists hold that sensory data are directly transformed into a conscious experience of emotion, the experience being the characteristic feeling of a particular emotion such as fear (Izard, 1971; Tomkins, 1962) (see Figure 2). Some cognitive-social theorists believe that emotion activation includes another step: self-perception of expressive behavior (Laird, 1984). According to this view, a stimulus event triggers neural processes that lead to expressive behavior, and the individual's perception of his or her own expressive behavior leads to emotion experience.

No current theory can explain the process whereby sensory information or perception gets transformed to feeling. Yet, everyone can testify to the existence of emotion feeling states. When the stimulus event is the loss of a loved one, the subsequent sensations, perceptions, and neural activity inevitably lead to sadness.

In a more substantive change, neo-Jamesian theorists hold that the sensory data in the feedback process is from voluntary muscle movements, primarily those involved in facial expressions. Hence sensory feedback is considered interchangeable with facial feedback. Some biosocial theorists have relegated sensory feedback from the car-

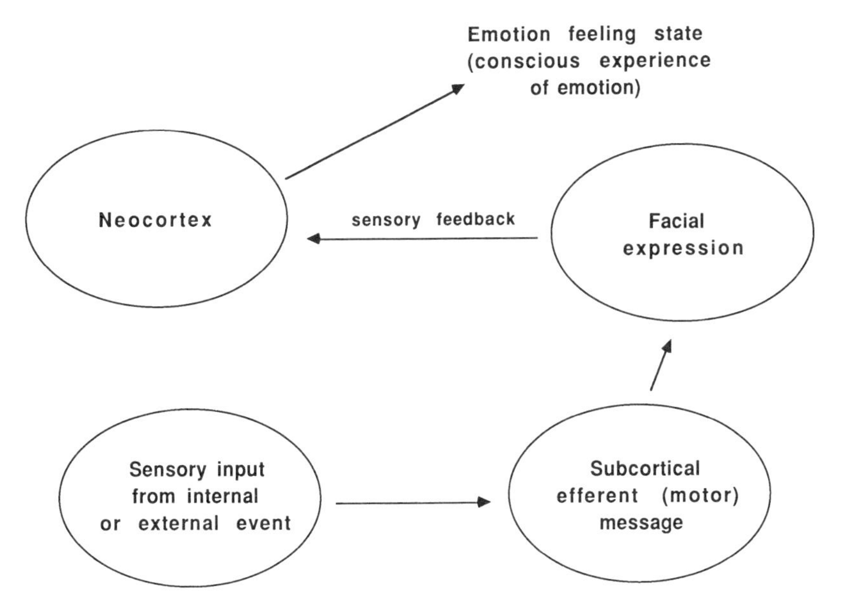

Figure 2. The facial feeback hypothesis of emotion activation.

diovascular, respiratory, and other ANS-innervated organs to a noncausal role in emotion activation (Izard, 1971; Tomkins, 1962). Recent evidence from spinal-cord-injured patients (Chwalisz et al., 1988) is consistent with this position. It shows that individuals deprived of sensory feedback from the neck down still experience emotions.

Thus some biosocial theorists hold that emotion is activated independently of the ANS and that activity of the ANS and the viscera is part of the individual's response to emotion (Izard, 1971; Tomkins, 1962). That the feedback from the ANS-innervated viscera is too slow to participate in rapid, automatic emotion activation mediated by the thalamoamygdala pathway favors biosocial theory. Feedback from the expressive behavior of the face is very fast and could participate in emotion activation via subcortical systems. That expressive behaviors undergo extensive developmental changes and culturally influenced modifications presents a problem for biosocial theory.

Cognitive Processes

In explaining emotion activation, cognitive processes such as appraisal and causal attribution are emphasized by constructivists, or social-cognitive theorists. (e.g., see Arnold, 1960; Lazarus, Kanner, & Folkman, 1980; Weiner & Graham, 1984). These theories are mainly concerned with emotions that follow from appraisal and attributional processes. A few of these theories hold that cognitive appraisal is a necessary antecedent of emotion.

Biosocial theory recognizes the causal role of appraisal and attributional processes, but it maintains that either uninterpreted sense data or minimally processed perceptual information can also lead to emotion without cognitive mediation. For example, on being knocked into a mud puddle on your way to an important meeting, either the pain alone or the frustrating sight of mud on your shoes and clothes might elicit anger immediately, regardless of the cause of the incident. Appraisal of the circumstances and a moment's reflection may lead to an interpretation of the cause of the event and to a change in emotion state, and such cognitive processes may attenuate or amplify the initial anger or change the anger to sadness. The hypothesis here is that we may react emotionally on the basis of sense impression or loosely organized perception before we reason why. However, the issue as to whether cognitive appraisal is a necessary antecedent of emotion experience remains controversial (Lazarus, 1984; Zajonc, 1984).

A Resolution of the Emotion Activation Issue

The controversy as to whether some cognitive process is a necessary antecedent of emotion may hinge on the definition of terms, particularly the definition of cognition. If we define cognition so broadly that it includes all levels or types of information processing, then cognition may be said to precede emotion activation. But such an overinclusive definition proffers a resolution of the issue by pronouncement and thus precludes empirical investigation.

One proposal is that we exclude from the concept of cognition all mental processes that do not involve mental representations based on learning or experience (Izard & Malatesta, 1987). This definition would exclude the electrochemical information processing in genes and body cells, direct responses to uninterpreted sensory data, and incompletely organized perceptions. Much, if not all, of precognitive information processing that activates emotions is automatic, unconscious, and mediated by subcortical structures and pathways (LeDoux, 1987). Cognition, as defined here, does not precede the formation of the affective preferences demonstrated by Zajonc (1980), the 3-week-old infant's smile in response to the high-pitched human voice (Wolff, 1969), or the 2-month-old's expression of anger in response to pain (Izard et al., 1983). It should be noted, however, that emotion experience in the preverbal infant must be inferred from expressive behavior, patterns of ANS activity, and functional relations between expressions and subsequent behaviors.

Consistent with the view that information processing is a broader concept than cognition, Hoffman (1985) described three increasingly complex modes of information processing that activate emotion, the first of which may be considered precognitive. Before presenting Hoffman's scheme, I shall describe yet another mode, even more basic than Hoffman's simplest type.

I propose that the most fundamental mode of information processing that activates emotion consists of direct transformations of sensory data or the direct activation of emotion pathways by physiological states. When an infant receives an inoculation, the injected serum acting on sensitive receptors results in sensations of pressure that register in the 2-month-old's consciousness as pain and the pain, in turn, is transformed into or activates anger (Izard et al., 1983; cf. Tomkins, 1963). Sensations of pain, such as when you stub your toe in the dark, may lead directly to anger without any appraisal of the stimulus or any inference about who left the object in your path. In this emotion activation sequence, there is no need to assume that cognitive processes intervened at any point. On the other hand, it is reasonable to assume that not only pain but other drive states that endure or reach a certain level of intensity activate emotion through direct transformations of sensory data or processes inherent in physiological states. In this context, Tomkins' (1962) suggestion that one emotion can activate another seems reasonable.

Hoffman's first mode of information processing is similar to the mode just described in that it is precognitive and primarily physical-sensory. The individual responds to certain stimuli emotionally as soon as certain physical features are detected and registered in consciousness. This mode involves a minimum of perceptual organization. An example is an unlearned emotional response, such as the 6-week-old infant's smile at a human face. Another example of such precognitive information processing is motor mimicry (see Hoffman, 1978). A young infant can mimic the mother's sadness expression, and sensory feedback from the expression could activate the experience of sadness in the infant.

Hoffman's second mode of information processing involves comparison processes and assumes the cognitive capacity for at least short-term memory. With this capacity an older infant can store an image or schema of an unconditioned or conditioned elicitor of emotion. Then, the infant is capable of comparing perceptions of other objects with that schema. If the newly perceived object matches the schema, positive emotions may be activated; mismatches may lead to negative emotions.

Hoffman's third type of information processing involves the cognitive processes required in deriving meaning from the stimulus. One such process is categorization. An individual forms a class or category by detecting the common features of a set of objects or events. When the individual detects stimulus features of an event common to a particular category, say, threat or danger, an emotion—in this case, fear—is activated. Another example of the third mode of information processing is appraisal. Through appraisal or evaluative processes, an individual may determine that an object is beneficial or harmful, enjoyable or frustrating (Arnold, 1960; Lazarus, 1984). Finally, inferences (or attributions) we make about the cause of an event may determine the quality of emotion that is activated (Weiner & Graham, 1984). Thus if a person next to you in the plane vomits because she is drunk, you may feel disgust, but if it's because she is air sick you may feel sorrow or pity.

The foregoing discussion suggests that a satisfactory model of emotion activation must be multimodal. Emotions can be activated by sensory processes, physiological states, motor mimicry, other sorts of precognitive information processing, and numerous cognitive processes including comparison, matching, appraisal, categorization, imagery, memory, and anticipation. Further, all emotion activation processes are influenced by a variety of internal and external factors, including homeostatic processes and ongoing emotion, cognition, and action.

The Structure of Emotions

This section of the paper concerns the structure of emotions and the following one the functions of emotions. This division of material does not assume a strict dichotomy. Thus in discussing structure it is not always possible to ignore function, but the separation should help us sort out the complex field of emotions.

Both biosocial and cognitive-social theories of emotions acknowledge that an emotion is a complex phenomenon. They generally agree that an emotion includes physiological functions, expressive behavior, and subjective experience and that each of these components is based on activity in the brain and nervous system. Some theorists, particularly of the cognitive-social persuasion, hold that an emotion also involves cognition, an appraisal or cognitive-evaluative process that triggers the emotion and determines, or contributes to, the subjective experience of the emotion.

It is important to remember that the components of an emotion stem from highly interdependent processes. The subjective experience of an emotion, as well as the physiological and expressive components, are manifestations of processes occurring in the brain, nervous system, and body. In this section, I shall discuss the structure of each of the components—physiological, expressive, and experiential—of an emotion.

The Physiological Component of Emotions

The physiological component of emotion has been a lively topic of research since Cannon (1927) challenged the James-Lange theory by showing that feedback from the viscera had little effect on emotional expression in animals. Cannon's studies and criticisms were flawed, however; among other things, he failed to discount the possible role of feedback from striated muscle systems of the face and body.

Physiological structures. Since the popularization of the James-Lange theory of emotion, the physiological component of the emotion traditionally has been identified as activity in the autonomic nervous system (ANS) and the visceral organs (e.g., heart, lungs) that it innervates. However, some current theorists hold that the neural basis of emotions resides in the central nervous system (CNS) and that the ANS is recruited by emotion to fulfill certain functions related to sustaining and regulating emotion experience and emotion-related behavior (Izard, 1977; Tomkins, 1962).

Neuroanatomical studies have shown that the CNS structures involved in emotion activation have afferent pathways to the ANS. For example, efferents from the amygdala to the hypothalamus may influence the ANS activity involved in defensive reactions (LeDoux, 1987). Further, there are connections between pathways innervating facial expression and the ANS (Hu, Dostrovsky, & Sessle, 1981).

Several studies have shown that patterns of ANS activity vary with the type of emotion being expressed. In one study trained adult subjects posed prototypical facial expressions of basic emotions while various physiological functions were being measured. The results showed that the emotions of joy, surprise, sadness, anger, disgust, and fear could be differentiated by their patterns of heart rate and skin temperature (Ekman, Levenson, & Friesen, 1983). A number of other studies have shown coherent relations among emotion experiences and ANS activity (e.g., Schwartz, Weinberger, & Singer, 1981).

Differential roles of the brain hemispheres. There is some evidence that the two brain hemispheres are involved differently in different emotions. Early evidence suggested that the right (or dominant) hemisphere may be more involved in mediating emotion than the left (e.g., Davidson, 1984). Later research using electroencephalography (EEG) has modified this initial conclusion and suggested that the right hemisphere may be more involved in processing negative emotions and the left hemisphere more involved in processing positive emotions (Fox & Davidson, 1984). An extensive series of studies on patients whose right and left hemispheres were disconnected for medical reasons indicated that the most stable finding from the research on differential hemispheric functioning is that the right hemisphere is more involved than the left in processing emotion information and mediating emotion experiences (Sperry, 1982). The significance of small differences in hemispheric participation (EEG activity) in positive versus negative emotions remains to be determined. Nevertheless, research on the physiological component of emotions must consider cortical activation as well as ANS activity.

The Expressive Component

The expressive component of emotion includes facial, vocal, postural, and gestural activity. Research indicates that facial expression is the most essential and stable aspect of emotion expression in human beings. Expressive behavior is mediated by phylogenetically old structures of the brain, suggesting that they may have served survival functions in the course of evolution.

Brain structures involved in emotion expressions and emotional behavior. There is a considerable body of evidence on the neural control of animals' emotional behavior, behavior that often has both signal value and instrumental functions. For example, the porcupine's erect bristles tell us the porcupine is threatened, and at the same time they discourage predators.

Emotion expressions involve limbic and forebrain structures and aspects of the peripheral nervous system. The facial and trigeminal nerves and receptors in facial muscles and skin are required for emotion expressions and sensory feedback.

Early studies of the neural basis of emotion expression showed that aggressive behavior can be elicited in a cat after its neocortex has been removed (Cannon, 1927) and suggested that the hypothalamus is a critical subcortical structure mediating aggression (Flynn, 1967). Further research showed that stimulation of the medial areas of the hypothalamus elicited affective attack or defensive behavior, whereas stimulation of lateral sites in the hypothalamus elicited predatory attack. Recent studies have suggested that the critical pathways in the hypothalamus are fibers of passage that have their cell bodies elsewhere. A review of this research indicates that rather than the hypothalamus, the central gray region of the midbrain and the substantia nigra may be the key structures mediating aggressive behavior in animals (LeDoux, 1987).

Neural pathways of facial expression. In human beings, and in many nonhuman primates, patterns of facial movements constitute the chief means of displaying emotion-specific signals. We have already noted that the facial expressions of seven basic emotions are innate and universal. Whereas research has provided much information on the neural basis of emotional behaviors (e.g., aggression) in animals, little is known about the brain structures that control facial expressions.

The peripheral pathways of emotion expression consist of the cranial nerves VII and V. Nerve VII, or the facial nerve, is the efferent pathway; it conveys motor messages from the brain to facial muscles. Nerve V, or the trigeminal nerve, is the afferent pathway that provides sensory data from movements of facial muscles and skin. The trigeminal nerve transmits the facial feedback that, according to some theorists, contributes to the activation and regulation of emotion experience. The impulses for this sensory feedback originate when movement stimulates the proprioceptors in muscle spindles and the mechanoreceptors in the skin.

Rinn (1984) noted that there are few spindles in facial muscles and, therefore, too few proprioceptors to provide the kind of patterned feedback required for the activation of specific emotions. However, Rinn overlooked the feedback from nociceptive and low-threshold mechanoreceptive neurons that project to facial skin. The skin is richly supplied with such receptors and the many branches of the trigeminal nerve appear quite adequate to the task of detecting and conveying the sensory impulses to the brain. The trigeminal nerve divides into three main branches, one for each major region of the face. Each of these regions contains muscle groups that make the appearance changes that constitute the emotion-specific components of the facial expressions of the emotions.

The innateness and universality of emotion expressions. Over a century ago, Darwin's (1872/1965) observations and correspondence with friends living in different parts of the world led him to conclude that certain emotion expressions are innate and universal, part of the basic structure of emotions. Contemporary crosscultural and developmental research has given strong support to Darwin's conclusion (Eibl-Eibesfeldt, 1972; Ekman, Sorenson, & Friesen, 1969; Izard, 1968, 1971; Izard, Huebner, Risser, McGinnes, & Dougherty, 1980). These studies showed that people in literate and preliterate cultures have a common understanding of the expressions of joy, surprise, sadness, anger, disgust, contempt, and fear. Other studies have suggested that interest and shyness may also be innate and universal (Kagan, Reznick, & Snidman, 1988; Langsdorf, Izard, Rayias, & Hembree, 1983). There is uncertainty about the universality of the expressions of interest and shyness, and no basis for believing there are universal expressions for shame and guilt, but a number of scientists believe that these four emotions are also biologically based and universal (see Izard, 1977).

The Experiential Component

There is general agreement that stimulus events and neural processes leading to an emotion result not only in physiological activities and expressive behavior, but also in subjective experience. Some biosocial theorists restrict the definition of an emotion experience to a feeling state and argue that it can obtain and function independently of cognition (e.g., Izard, 1977; Zajonc, 1980). Experiences that involve feeling and cognition are viewed as affective-cognitive structures.

Cognitive-social theorists view the experiential component of emotion as having a cognitive aspect. Kagan (1984) holds that the infant has to perceive or detect the underlying physiological changes before it can experience feeling states. He believes that upon detection, the infant's perceived change in feeling state is motivational and that it invites a cognitive judgment or interpretation of its cause. Lewis and Michalson (1983) maintain that emotion experiences occur as the result of the cognitive interpretations and evaluations of physiological states and expressions. Further, they argue that the infant must have a concept of self before emotion can be experienced. In their view, children have to be able to develop a fairly complex cognitive structure before they can feel or experience emotion. The issue regarding the possibility of independence of emotion feeling states and cognition remains unresolved, but it is widely agreed that emotion-feeling states and cognitive processes are frequently, if not typically, highly interactive.

The experiential component of emotion is at once the easiest and most difficult to explain. It is easy in that it is the aspect of emotion that acquires consciousness. It is what we feel in contentment and involvement and during the challenges and frustrations of daily life. Emotion experience is difficult to define and explain because it is ultimately a private matter. Attempts to communicate about emotion experiences are thwarted by the seeming inadequacy of language to describe precisely how we feel. There are few instances where feelings and words are perfectly matched, where a word gives a complete sense of the feeling we are experiencing.

Unfortunately, emotion experiences do not lend themselves to objective measurement. All research on emotion experiences ultimately depends on self-reports and these are imprecise. Yet, most students of emotions, whether philosopher or neuroscientist, ultimately want to explain emotion experience.

Biological structures: The neural basis of emotion experience. Very little is known about the neural basis of emotion experiences. As we discussed in the section on emotion activation, the James-Lange tradition and some cognitive-social theorists hold that sensory feedback from ANS activity provides the physiological basis for the subjective experience of emotion. Recent critical reviews have shown that there is little evidence to support this position (Chwalisz et al., 1988; LeDoux, 1987). As already noted, there is some evidence to support the hypothesis that sensory feedback from facial expression contributes to emotion experience (see Izard, 1988 for a review), but not much is known about the neural connections between expressions and the central pathways that mediate emotion.

In recent years, cognitive models of emotion experience have influenced conceptions of the neural basis of emotion (LeDoux, 1987). Explanations of emotions in terms of appraisal and attributional processes led some to posit that conscious experiences of emotions derive from the cognitive processes that underlie language. This led to the hypothesis that emotion experiences involve interactions between limbic forebrain areas and the areas of the neocortex that mediate language and language-based cognitive systems (LeDoux, 1987).

Emotion experiences as feeling states. There are several problems with the conclusion that emotion experiences are mediated by language-based cognitive systems and their neural substrates. First, there is now robust evidence for unconscious cognitive processes (Kihlstrom, 1987), some of which could surely contribute to emotion activation. Second, there are discrete emotion expressions and emotion-related behaviors in infants long before they acquire language (Izard et al., 1980). Third, there is the possibility that emotion experience is essentially a feeling state or quality of consciousness that can be independent of higher order cognitive processes and language. This notion is supported by the research on discrete emotion expressions and their functions in the preverbal infant and in congenitally deaf or blind children before they acquire speech (cf. Dumas, 1948). It seems unwarranted to conclude that animals and humans without language—infants and preverbal blind or deaf children—have no emotion experiences. However, the investigation of emotion experiences remains dependent on language (self-report), and the hypothesis that areas of the brain that mediate language also mediate emotion experiences should be pursued.

If we accept the view of some biosocial theorists that emotion experience is essentially a feeling state or quality of consciousness, then we can separate emotion experience and cognition. In this framework, emotion experience, as feeling, can exist in consciousness and influence cognition and action without being labeled and articulated. Thus emotion experience as feeling can derive from several sources, language-based cognition being one of them.

Both cognitive (Arnold, 1960; Lang, 1984; Plutchik, 1980) and biosocial theorists (Campos, Barrett, Lamb, Goldsmith, & Stenberg, 1983; Izard, 1977) have emphasized that *emotions include action tendencies.* Conceivably these action tendencies could derive from the physiological function, expression, or experience. Action tendencies that result in automatic responses to emotion feelings (e.g., tensing muscles in anger, loss of muscle tone in sadness) may operate at an unconscious level, whereas action tendencies that influence voluntary actions (e.g., aggression or retreat, verbalization of hostility or verbalization of compliance) operate at the conscious level and are part of emotion experiences.

Emotion-based action tendencies in the young infant typically materialize as loosely organized movements of the head, arms, and legs. The neocortical structures and pathways responsible for inhibiting and regulating actions are not sufficiently mature in early development to control emotion-driven action tendencies. With increasing maturation, the neocortex becomes capable of facilitating or inhibiting actions. With increasing capacity for cortical control, the matter of whether emotion-driven action tendencies are actualized in exploratory, affectionate, fearful, or aggressive behaviors depends on the strength of the tendency, the evaluation of the event and the consequences of action, and the overall strategy of adaptation. Research on the electromyography of somatic muscles of the face and body in response to emotion-eliciting events should increase our understanding of emotion feeling states (Fridlund, Schwartz, & Fowler, 1984; Sirota, Schwartz, & Kristeller, 1987).

A number of studies, which will be reviewed later, have shown that induced emotions influence perception, learning, memory, and creative problem solving. This robust evidence for the effects of emotion on perceptual and cognitive processes clearly indicate that *emotion experiences are rich sources of cues for cognition* that help determine the contents and operations of consciousness.

The Functions of Emotions

Do emotions influence perception, cognition, social relations, and actions? Typically, the literature on the subject describes the role of emotion as though a given emotion is a unitary or unidimensional process. A close look at the matter reveals that in discussions of the functions of emotions the focus is usually on the phenomenological aspect of emotion (Arnold, 1960; Plutchik, 1980; Tomkins, 1962). Here, I shall try to separate the functions of emotions in terms of the three structural components: physiological, expressive, and experiential. Just as it was not possible to make a clean dichotomy between structure and function, it will not be possible to sort functions neatly according to the three separate components. Each component of an emotion does have some distinct functions, but organizing functions by components should not make us lose sight of the holistic and systemic nature of emotions.

The Functions of the Physiological Component

The ANS-mediated physiological activity that accompanies emotion states can be considered as part of the individual's effort to adapt and cope. Higher heart rate and increased respiration can facilitate the motor activities required for aggressive or defensive action in anger- or fear-eliciting situations. Heart-rate deceleration at the onset of interest may reflect physiological quieting that facilitates information processing.

It is easy to understand the adaptiveness of anger- or fear-related change in the cardiovascular system where the situation calls for defense of life and limb or escape from imminent danger. It is not so easy to understand it in a situation such as a confrontation with an irate spouse, client, or supervisor. In the latter type of situation, adaptiveness appears to follow from effective regulation of emotion experience and expression, which in turn helps regulate physiological processes.

That the physiological processes associated with emotion require regulation does not mean that they are not inherently adaptive. Among other things, the ANS activity and the activity of hormones and other neurotransmitters are probably essential to maintaining emotion-driven cognition and action over time. Further, changes in patterns of ANS activity, in accordance with changes in specific emotions, may be essential to adaptive functioning. Evidence shows that the interest expression in infants is associated with heart-rate deceleration (Langsdorf et al., 1983). Adaptation to events and situations that elicit interest require quite a different behavioral strategy than do situations that elicit fear. The heart-rate deceleration and quieting of internal organs in interest should maximize intake and cognitive processing of information, whereas heart-rate acceleration in fear prepares us to cope by more active means, whether through cognitive processes, gross motor actions, verbalizations, or various combinations of these behaviors.

The Functions of Emotion Expressions

Emotion expressions have three major functions: (a) they contribute to the activation and regulation of emotion experiences; (b) they communicate something about our internal states and intentions to others; and (c) they activate emotions in others, a process that can help account for empathy and altruistic behavior.

Emotion expressions contribute to the activation and regulation of emotion experiences. In his famous volume *The Expressions of Emotions in Man and Animals,* Darwin (1872/1965) clearly revealed his belief that even voluntary emotion expression evoked emotion feeling. He wrote, "Even the simulation [expression] of an emotion tends to arouse it in our minds" (p. 365). Thus Darwin's idea suggested that sensations created by the movements of expressive behavior activate, or contribute to the activation, of emotion feeling.

About 20 experiments have tested some version of a facial-feedback hypothesis of the activation of emotion feelings (Laird, 1984). Careful scrutiny of these experiments, including meta-analyses of the statistics (Izard, 1988; Matsumoto, 1987; Winton, 1986), indicates that they are of two types. In one type, the subjects, at the experimenter's request, move their facial muscles so as to form an emotion expression without being aware that the movements result in such a pattern. The effects of the presumed emotion feeling are measured in various ways. In the other type, the subjects are motivated to initiate expressive behavior or regulate event-elicited expressive behavior in the interest of some goal. The meta-analyses of studies of both types indicate that the first type—based on subject-blind, experimenter manipulated, facial movements—has demonstrated a weak, though statistically significant, effect. This effect has not been clearly shown to be emotion-specific. The second type, involving motivated, self-initiated, or self-managed expression, has proved considerably more effective in regulating emotion experiences. Experiments of this type have provided substantial evidence that intentional management of facial expression contributes to the regulation (and perhaps activation) of emotion experiences. However, extant evidence relates not to specific emotion feelings but to the broad classes of positive and negative emotion states.

So, there is some scientific support for the old advice to "smile when you feel blue" and "whistle a happy tune when you're afraid." The research on intentional expressive behavior as a mode of emotion regulation has significant implications for child rearing and psychotherapy.

Darwin was even more persuasive when speaking specifically of the regulation of emotion experience by self-initiated expressive behavior. He wrote:

> The free expression by outward signs of an emotion intensifies it. On the other hand, the repression, as far as this is possible, of all outward signs softens our emotions. He who gives way to violent gestures will increase his rage; he who does not control the signs of fear will experience fear in a greater degree (Darwin, 1872/1965, p. 365).

Although a limited set of facial expressions are preprogrammed or inborn, so is their control and modifiability and hence their potential for regulating emotion feelings. Some of the experiments on motivated, self-initiated expressive behaviors have shown that if you can control your facial expression during moments of pain you will actually experience less pain. This finding was based on measures of ANS activity as well as reports of the conscious feeling of pain (Lanzetta, Cartwright-Smith, & Kleck, 1976).

Emotion expressions communicate internal states. Nowhere is the social-communication function of emotion expressions more evident than in infancy. Long before the infants have command of a single word, much less a thought in their head, they can send a wide variety of messages through their facial expressions. Virtually all the facial movements necessary for the expression of the basic emotions are present before birth (Oster, 1978).

I developed an anatomically based system for coding the separate facial muscle movements hypothesized to be signals of emotions (Izard, 1979). This is an objective system that requires coders to assign numbers to discrete appearance changes in three different regions of the face. Using this system we found that the facial expression of pain and the expressions of interest, the newborn smile, and disgust are present at birth, the social smile by 3 or 4 weeks, sadness and anger by about 2 months, and fear by 6 or 7 months. The facial expressions of anger in infants have the same facial muscle actions as adult expressions. Informal observations suggest that behaviors indicative of shyness appear by about 4 months and guilt behaviors by about 2 years.

Each of the infant's facial expressions communicates a distinct message to the caregiver. Indeed, the expressive behaviors are the infants' primary means of signaling their internal states and of becoming engaged in the family and human community. Emotion expressions help form the foundation for social relationships and social development. Infants' expressions of the positive emotions obtain the caregivers' attention. The resulting social and affectionate exchange between caregivers and infants contributes significantly to the parent-infant attachment or love relationship. It also provides stimulation that appears to be necessary for physically and mentally healthy development (Greenspan & Porges, 1985). On the other hand, infants' expressions of negative emotions provide their caregivers with specific information that guides them in the amelioration of stress and the prevention of trauma. Evidence suggests that mothers respond differently to their infants' expressions of sadness, anger, and pain (Huebner & Izard, 1988).

Emotion expressions motivate others to respond. Studies have shown that 1- and 3-day-old infants cry in response to another infant's cry but not to a computer-generated sound that simulates crying (Sagi & Hoffman, 1976). Other studies have shown that infants of 2 or 3 months' age respond quite differently to different expressions by the mother (Haviland & Lelwica, 1987). A naturalistic study of the effects of infants' reduced expressiveness showed that the emotion expressions of Down's Syndrome infants are disturbing to their parents, sometimes profoundly so (Emde, Katz, & Thorpe, 1978). An infant's emotion expressions also affect the mother's physiological responses (Weisenfeld & Klorman, 1978). Main, Tomasini, and

Tolan (1979) showed that infants of mothers who were more emotionally expressive were more likely to be classified as secure (rather than insecure) in their relationship with their mother. A number of experiments have demonstrated that the information an infant obtains from the mother's facial expressions mediates or regulates a variety of infant behaviors (Klinnert, Campos, Sorce, Emde, & Svejda, 1983). For example, most infants will cross a modified visual cliff if their mother stands on the opposite side and smiles, but none will cross if she expresses fear.

Facial expressions, particularly of sadness, may facilitate empathy and altruistic behavior. Darwin thought facial expressions evoked empathy and concluded that expression-induced empathy was inborn. His evidence came from informal experiments in which he observed his 5-month-old son match the simulated expressions of others. He said:

> . . . I was convinced that he understood a smile and received pleasure from seeing one, answering it by another, at much too early an age to have learnt anything by experience. . . . When five months old, his nurse pretended to cry, and I saw that his face instantly assumed a melancholy expression, with the corners of the mouth strongly depressed . . . (Darwin, 1872/1965, p. 358).

Recently, researchers systematically and objectively coded 9-month-old infants' sadness expressions in response to their mothers' sadness expressions. The results of the study showed that when the mothers maintained the sadness expression, the infants showed a significant decrease in exploratory play (see Figure 3). The infants also showed more sadness expressions and gazed less at their mothers.

It appears that the expression and feeling of sadness induced by another person's sadness expression provides the motivation for altruistic behavior (Hoffman, 1978). One study showed that infants under 2 years of age responded to their mothers' real or simulated expressions of sadness or distress with efforts to make reparations and provide help (Zahn-Waxler, Radke-Yarrow, & King, 1979).

Functions of Emotion Experiences

Psychologists who adopt a strong behavioristic position deny that emotion experiences are matters for scientific inquiry. In contrast, some biosocial theories hold that emotion feelings must be studied because they are the primary factors in organizing and motivating human behavior. Most of the functions I have attributed to emotion

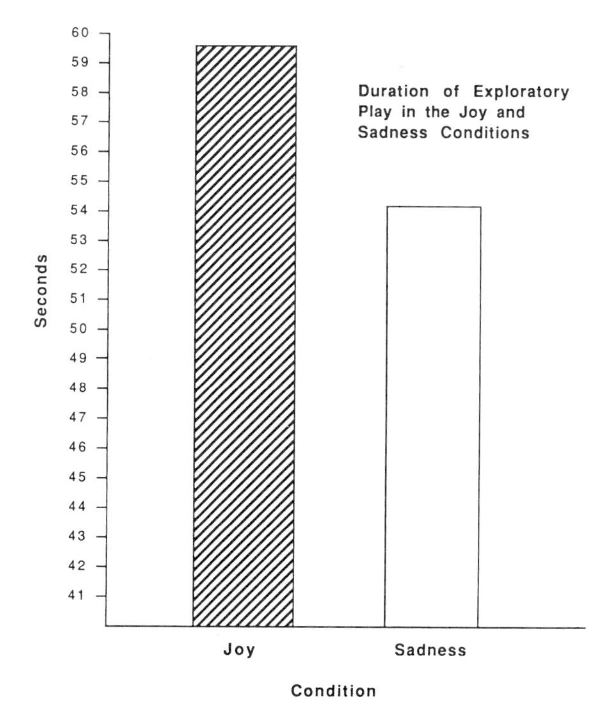

Figure 3. Mother's sadness decreases exploratory play in her infant. Adapted from Termine and Izard (1988) with permission.

expression, such as empathy and altruism, are dependent on the organizing and motivating properties of underlying emotion feelings.

Several lines of research show that a concept of emotion experience as a cause of cognitive and behavioral processes is critical in the explanation of a number of phenomena. Discussion of these phenomena should clarify some of the significant functions of the experiential component of emotion. In this discussion, an emotion experience is defined as the particular quality of consciousness or feeling characteristic of a specific emotion, for example, the feeling that characterizes joy or sadness.

Emotion experiences as a common bond among human beings. Research has shown that people in widely different literate and preliterate cultures not only recognize basic emotion expressions, they characterize and label them with semantically equivalent terms (Ekman, Friesen, & Ellsworth, 1972; Izard, 1971). People everywhere attach similar meanings to basic emotions and describe the feeling of anger or fear in the same way. It seems reasonable to assume that the common feeling state of a given emotion contributes to the generation of cues for the cognitive processes that result in emotion concepts that are similar across cultures. Of course, if people include contextual factors in their description of an emotion experience, then there will be differences across cultures. In some cultures fear of spirits and curses is real, in others not. Including contextual factors involves causes and consequences of the emotion. Even individuals within cultures learn to be afraid of quite different things—great heights frighten some people, confinement in close quarters frightens others. But the feeling of fear is the same, and it always motivates cognitive processes and actions relating to escape from danger and finding physical or psychological safety and security.

Emotion feelings give meaning to emotion expressions. Most of the functions of emotion expressions are dependent on emotion feelings. The messages conveyed by expressive behavior relate to internal feelings as well as to external events. A mother's fear expression not only conveys her feelings but alerts her children to scan the situation for signs of danger.

Expressive behaviors are powerful stimuli in learning and conditioning. One study showed that laboratory-reared monkeys that showed no fear of snakes quickly show fear and avoidance after seeing their wild-reared mother's expressive behavior in response to the snake. The wild-reared monkeys displayed fear and avoidance behaviors after more than 15 years without exposure to snakes (Mineka, Davidson, Cook, & Keir, 1984). This seems difficult to explain without assuming that the sight of the snake triggered a powerful feeling state that motivated escape.

Similarly, the role of emotion expression in facilitating empathy is related to the underlying feeling. A person's expression of distress or sadness signals the person's feeling or internal state. The observer may assume the same expression, but if the expression is not associated with the appropriate feeling, there will be no motivation to help (cf. Hoffman, 1978). The helping behavior alleviates the person's plight as well as the empathic distress and sadness of the helper.

Emotion experiences influence perception and cognition. Several lines of research have shown that induced emotion affects perception, learning, and memory. In one study (Izard, Wehmer, Livsey, & Jennings, 1965) subjects were made happy or angry and then shown happy or angry faces and friendly or hostile interpersonal scenes in a stereoscope. Happy subjects perceived more happy faces and friendly interpersonal scenes, and angry subjects perceived more angry faces and hostile interpersonal scenes. In this case, emotion altered the basic perceptual process. Every time the subjects looked into the stereoscope, their left eye was exposed to one type of expression and their right eye to another type. For a subject to report seeing a happy or angry expression, the binocular rivalry set up by the disparate information in the two visual fields had to be resolved through unconscious cognitive processes. Apparently, the induced emotion determined the direction of this resolution. If this is so, it is scientific evidence for the folklore that tells us that when happy we see the world through rose-colored glasses.

A recent experiment extended the findings of the stereoscope study. The experimenters (Forgas & Bower, 1987) used bogus feedback and role-playing techniques to induce happiness or sadness. Subjects were then given happy and sad information about fictional persons and were later asked to give their impressions and make some judgments about the fictional characters. Overall, happy subjects made more favorable impressions and positive judgments than did sad subjects; the happy mood had a greater effect than the sad mood. As in earlier studies, both cued recall and recognition memory were superior for mood-congruent material—when the subject's mood matched the information being learned. The authors concluded that moods influence our impressions and judgments about people in everyday life and that future research should be directed toward understanding these processes in different social contexts.

Some well-supported conclusions follow from the recent research on emotions and cognition. Emotions influence perceptual processes, even determining what we perceive. Learning while in a particular mood means that material congruent with that mood will be processed in such a way that it is better remembered than incongruous material. Mood-induced selective perception and learning can shape our judgments about people. Further, when in a sad mood you recall more sad childhood events and fewer pleasant ones than when in a happy mood (Bower, 1981). This sort of mood-congruency effect may have practical implications for understanding and treating depression. The sad mood that characterizes depressed individuals may cause them to recall and ruminate over sad events of the past. Such cognition may in turn exacerbate the depression.

Positive emotion feelings facilitate empathy and altruism. Isen (1984) and her colleagues conducted an extensive series of studies that showed that relatively small favors or bits of good luck (like finding money in a coin telephone or getting an unexpected gift) induce positive emotion in people. Such positive emotion regularly changes the subjects' subsequent behavior in the direction of empathy and altruism (Isen, Daubman, & Norwicki, 1987).

Positive emotion increases creativity. Several studies have demonstrated that positive emotion facilitates cognitive processes such as thinking, remembering, categorizing, and creative problem solving (Isen & Daubman, 1984; Izard et al., 1965). One of these studies showed that positive emotion increased the likelihood of seeing relations among objects, resulting in the placement of more stimuli in a particular category. Another study showed that positive emotion enhanced creative problem solving by enabling subjects to see relations among objects that would otherwise go unnoticed.

In one of these studies (Izard et al., 1965), positive and negative emotions were induced by having subjects interact with an actress who was either happy and encouraging or hostile and critical. Following the emotion-induction episode, subjects who interacted with the actress as she role-played a friendly, encouraging person perceived the experimenter more favorably and performed better on measures of intellectual functioning and creativity. For example, as compared to subjects in the negative emotion condition, those in the positive emotion condition were able to name more uses for common objects, an ability associated with creative problem solving. In another series of studies (Isen et al., 1987), positive emotion induced with a few minutes of an amusing film or a gift of a small bag of candy caused subjects to perforın more effectively on intellectural and creative problem-solving tasks. For example, given a box of tacks, a candle, and a book of matches, subjects in the positive emotion condition were more likely to figure out how to attach the candle to the wall (corkboard) in such a way that it would not drip on the floor. (They removed the tacks from the box, put the candle in it, and tacked the box to the wall.)

A number of studies have shown that these effects of positive emotion on thinking, memory, and action can be demonstrated in preschool and older children. In one study (Nasby & Yando, 1982), fifth-grade children were asked to recall and visualize an experience that made them happy, sad, or angry. Following the emotion induction, they were asked to learn a list of words that had either positive or negative connotation. After the learning task, the emotion induction task was repeated and memory tests administered. The results showed that a happy mood during learning or during the memory test facilitated the recall of positive words. Sad and angry moods decreased memory for positive words, and the angry mood increased memory for negative words.

Explaining the functions of emotion experiences. There are two kinds of factors that contribute to the salubrious effects of positive emotion on perception, learning, creative problem solving, and prosocial behavior. Two factors, emphasized by cognitive-social theorists, relate to cognitive processes. Positive emotion cues positive material in memory, and positive material in memory is more extensive than neutral and negative material (Isen, Shalker, Clark, & Karp, 1978). The second set of factors, emphasized by biosocial theorists, relate to the intrinsic motivational and organizational influences of emotion and to the particular characteristics of the subjective experience of positive emotion. For example, they maintain that the experience of joy is characterized by heightened self-esteem and self-confidence. These qualities of consciousness increase openness to information and flexibility of mental processes. Biosocial theorists see the positive emotion that is induced by experimental manipulations and by experimental tasks as including the emotion of interest as well as enjoyment. The subjective experience of interest is characterized by curiosity and the desire to explore and learn. Even in young infants, stimuli that elicit greater amounts of interest expression also elicit the most attention (Langsdorf et al., 1983).

In summary, biosocial theories hold that the motivational and organizational functions of the positive emotions of interest and enjoyment account for their facilitative effects on perception, cognition, and action. However, the explanatory concepts emphasized by biosocial and cognitive-social theories are not contradictory nor mutually exclusive.

Emotions, Motivation, and Adaptation

The results of many of the experiments already discussed indicate that emotions have motivational properties. Perhaps the most convincing demonstrations of emotions as motivations come from the studies showing that emotions influence perception, learning, and memory, and empathic, altruistic, and creative actions. Nevertheless, judgments of the importance of emotions in human motivation vary widely among cognitive-social and biosocial theories.

Cognitive-social theories of emotion tend to treat emotions as responses or effects (dependent variables), whereas biosocial theories see emotions as causes and effects (independent and dependent variables). Cognitive-social theories seek to explain how cognitive and social processes bring about emotions. Biosocial theories place more emphasis on explaining how emotions influence perception, cognition, and action.

Emotions as adaptive and emotions as disorganizing. Traditionally, emotions have been viewed as disorganizing and disrupting (Cannon, 1927). This tradition was fueled by the early studies of "emergency emotions" such as rage and panic. This approach also viewed emotions as transient, episodic states that needed to be brought under control or eliminated as rapidly as possible. Most of us would agree that rage and panic are disruptive and that they can lead to behaviors that prove to be maladaptive, even fatal. However, this view did not consider emotions at low or moderate levels of intensity or the possibility that emotion feeling states are continuous in consciousness rather than transient.

Some of the motivational and organizational functions of emotion were described more than 40 years ago (Leeper, 1948), but it was not until 20 years later that this view began to emerge as a significant force in psychology. A substantial body of crosscultural and developmental data gave impetus to this change. In brief, these data showed that certain emotion expressions were indeed innate and universal (Ekman, Sorenson, & Friesen, 1969; Izard, 1968, 1971), as Darwin (1872/1965) concluded 117 years ago, and that emotion expressions serve critical functions in mother-infant communication and attachment (see Campos, Barrett, Lamb, Goldsmith, & Stenberg, 1983; and Izard & Malatesta, 1987, for reviews). The developmental studies showed, for example, that infants as young as 3 months of age responded with negative emotion expressions and withdrawal-like behaviors when a mother stopped playing with them and assumed an expressionless and silent "poker face" (Tronick, Ricks, & Cohn, 1982). As discussed in a preceding section, other studies have shown that inducing subjects to feel positive emotions leads them to be more empathic, altruistic, and creative. These studies are powerful and convincing demonstrations that emotions motivate and organize behaviors.

Limitations of the Adaptiveness of Emotions

Although the current trend in psychology seems to favor viewing emotions as having motivating, organizing, and adaptive functions, the study of emotions as response syndromes should not be neglected. Extreme anger and fear can bring about large changes in the activities of internal organs innervated by the ANS (Ekman et al., 1983; Rusalova et al., 1975). Some evidence suggests that periodic SNS-adrenal-medulary arousal may facilitate toughening up or the development of resistance to mental and physical disorders, while repeated SNS-adrenal-cortical arousal may have adverse effects. It may be that these types of arousal correspond to different types of intense emotion or to the same emotion under different circumstances. Anger in situations where its expression is threatening may endanger health, whereas anger in situations where its expression has constructive effects and is rewarding may be beneficial to health and well-being. That intense emotions under certain conditions have adverse effects does not mean that the basic motivational and organizational functions of emotions are maladaptive. Rather, it may indicate that there are deficiencies in the cognitive and motor processes that trigger and regulate emotions.

It is also reasonable to question whether emotions always motivate adaptive behaviors. Are there limits to their adaptiveness? An extreme view holds that even in so-called emotional disorders or psychopathology, emotions are not at fault. Rather, the problems reside in what we think and do, in cognitions and behaviors (Mowrer, 1960). For example, if we decide to break our moral code, we *should* feel guilt. The guilt is adaptive in that it motivates us to make amends. What is maladaptive is our decision to be immoral and our immoral behavior. Similarly, if we lose self-esteem because we did not study or work hard enough, we *should* feel sadness. This emotion can motivate us to work our way out of trouble. And if we are ashamed because we did not know an answer or have a skill we needed, the feeling of shame, or anticipation of it, can motivate us to self-improvement (Izard & Schwartz, 1986; cf. Tomkins, 1963). In this framework, psychological problems or disorders arise because the individual fails to respond appropriately to the emotion's motivational cues while the emotion is still at low or moderate intensity. Either repeated failures to respond or inappropriate responses to the inherently adaptive motivational aspects of emotions may mean that a troublesome situation will eventually amplify the emotion to such an extreme that its adaptive functions cannot be engaged.

Emotions, Temperament, and Personality

Most theorists agree that emotion thresholds and emotion responsiveness are part of the infrastructure of temperament and personality. However, there has been little empirical research on the relations among measures of emotions, dimensions of temperament, and personality traits.

Emotions and Temperament

Most theories of temperament define at least one dimension of temperament in terms of emotion. Two theories maintain that negative emotions form the core of one of the basic and stable dimensions of temperament (Buss & Plomin, 1984; Thomas & Chess, 1977). Others (e.g., Rothbart & Derryberry, 1981) hold that some dimensions of temperament can be accounted for in terms of positive emotions whereas others relate to negative emotions. One theory (Goldsmith & Campos, 1982) suggests that each of the dimensions of temperament is rooted in a particular discrete emotion and that temperamental dimensions form the emotional substrate of personality characteristics. Thus temperamental proneness to anger influences the development of aggressiveness, the emotion of interest accounts for temperamental persistence, and so on (see Goldsmith, et al.). These are interesting theoretical propositions, but there is little empirical support for them.

Emotions and Personality

A number of major personality theories, like theories of termperament, identify dimensions or traits of personality in terms of emotions. For example, Eysenck (1952) proposed three fundamental dimensions of personality: extraversion/introversion, neuroticism, and psychoticism. Neuroticism can be viewed as emotionality, defined, as in temperament theory, as nonspecific, negative, emotional responsiveness. Emotionality, so defined, appears as a trait in other personality theories. Extraversion/introversion can also be viewed as sociability, another dimension or trait common to several theories of personality. Sociability can also be related to emotion (interest, as expressed toward people, and shyness). Although these personality traits of emotionality and sociability have not been analyzed in terms of specific emotions, numerous empirical studies testify to their stability and validity in explaining human behaviors.

Several studies have shown that measures of positive emotionality and negative emotionality are independent, not inversely related, and have stability over time (Diener & Emmons, 1984). Further, it has been shown that positive and negative emotionality have different relations with symptoms of psychological disorders. For example, negative emotionality correlates positively with panic attack, panic-associated symptoms, and obsessive-compulsive symptoms, whereas positive emotionality correlates negatively with these phenomena (Watson & Tellegen, 1985). Global measures of positive emotionality (Watson, 1988) as well as measures of discrete positive emotions (Blumberg & Izard, 1986) help distinguish between anxiety and depression. Although several of the same negative emotions characterize both of these disorders, a lack of positive emotion experiences is more characteristic of depression than of anxiety.

The Continuity of Emotion Expressiveness

A few studies have shown that specific emotions, identified in terms of expressive behavior and physiological functions, have trait-like stability. Washburn's (1929) classic study showed stability of smiling and laughing from the first to second year of life.

Four studies have shown stability of wariness or fear responses. Scarr and Salapatek (1970) found short-term (2-month interval) stability in fear expression in infants 6 to 18 months of age. Bayley (1956) and Bronson (1972) showed that wariness or fear of strangers in infancy predicted fear or shyness in preschool years, and Kagan and Moss (1962) found that this relation held from infancy to adulthood.

In the longitudinal study of infants' responses to the pain of DPT inoculations (Izard et al., 1987), affect expressions were identified with the Max and Affex anatomically-based, objective coding systems (Izard, 1979; Izard et al., 1983). Anger expression indexes aggregated (averaged) for DPTs 1, 2, and 3 at ages 2, 4, and 6 months predicted anger expression in the DPT inoculation situation at 19 months of age ($R = .53$). Similar results were obtained for the sadness expression ($R = .55$).

Malatesta and Haviland's (1982) study of mother-infant interaction and separation found that infants' expressions at 3 to 6 months were predictors of infant emotion expressive patterns at 9 to 12 months. Emotion expression patterns have also shown continuity from 13 to 18 months of age during brief mother–infant separation (Hyson & Izard, 1985). The Time 1–Time 2 correlations were .61, .90, .53, and .90 for interest, anger, blends, and total negative emotion expression, respectively (Hyson & Izard, 1985).

Conclusion

Recent research in neuroscience and developmental psychology suggests that emotions can be activated automatically and unconsciously in subcortical pathways. Such precognitive information processing may be continuous, and the resulting emotion states may influence the many perceptual-cognitive processes that activate emotions through corticolimbic pathways.

Both types of emotion activation have important implications for the role of emotions in cognition and action. Subcortical, automatic information processing may provide the primitive data for immediate emotional response, whereas corticolimbic, higher order cognitive information processing yields the evaluations and attributions necessary for the appropriate emotions and coping strategy in a complex situation.

Emotions have physiological, expressive, and experiential components, and each component can be studied in terms of its structure and functions. The physiological component influences the intensity and duration of felt emotion, expressions serve communicative and sociomotivational functions, and emotion experiences (feeling states) influence cognition and action.

Discrete emotion concepts and variables have become part of the mainstream of developmental, social, and personality psychology. They are represented in psychophysiological research and are beginning to find their way into clinical investigations. They have even penetrated the cognitive sciences and the traditional center of experimental psychology—perception, learning, and memory. In the past two decades, research has shown that certain emotion expressions are innate, universal, and have significant functions in infant development and infant–caregiver relations, and that there are stable individual differences in emotion expressiveness. Emotion states influence what we perceive, learn, and remember, and they are implicated in the development of empathic, altruistic, and moral behavior and of basic personality traits.

References

Arnold, M. B. (1960). *Emotion and personality: Vol. 1. Psychological aspects.* New York: Columbia University Press.

Ax, A. F. (1953). The physiological differentiation between fear and anger in humans. *Psychosomatic Medicine, 15,* 433-442.

Bayley, N. (1956). Individual patterns of development. *Child Development, 27,* 45-74.

Beck, A. T. (1976). *Cognitive therapy and the emotional disorders.* New York: International Universities Press, Inc.

Blumberg, S. H., & Izard, C. E. (1986). Discriminating patterns of emotions in 10- and 11-year-old children's anxiety and depression. *Journal of Personality and Social Psychology, 51*(4), 852-857.

Bower, G. H. (1981). Emotional mood and memory. *American Psychologist, 36*(2), 129-148.

Bronson, G. W. (1972). Infants' reactions to unfamiliar persons and novel objects. *Monographs of the Society for Research in Child Development, 37*(3, Serial No. 148).

Buss, D. M., & Plomin, R. (1984). *Temperament: Early developing personality traits.* Hillsdale, NJ: Erlbaum.

Campos, J. J., Barrett, K. C., Lamb, M. E., Goldsmith, H. H., & Stenberg, C. (1983). Socioemotional development. In M. M. Haith & J. J. Campos (Eds.), *Handbook of child psychology: Vol. 2. Infancy and developmental psychobiology* (pp. 783-915). New York: Wiley.

Cannon, W. B. (1927). The James-Lange theory of emotions: A critical examination and an alternative theory. *American Journal of Psychology, 39,* 106-124.

Chwalisz, K., Diener, E., & Gallagher, D. (1988). Autonomic arousal feedback and emotional experience: Evidence from the spinal cord injured. *Journal of Personality and Social Psychology, 54*(5), 820-828.

Darwin, C. R. (1965). *The expression of emotions in man and animals.* London: John Murray; Chicago: University of Chicago Press. (Originally published in 1872).

Davidson, R. J. (1984). Affect, cognition, and hemispheric specialization. In C. E. Izard, J. Kagan, & R. B. Zajonc (Eds.), *Emotions, cognition, and behavior* (pp. 320-365). New York: Cambridge University Press.

Diener, E., & Emmons, R. A. (1984). The independence of positive and negative affect. *Journal of Personality and Social Psychology, 47,* 1105-1117.

Dienstbier, R. A. (in press). Arousal and physiological toughness: Implications for mental and physical health. *Psychological Review.* Manuscript submitted for publication.

Duffy, E. (1941). An explanation of "emotional" phenomena without the use of the concept "emotion." *Journal of General Psychology, 25,* 283-293.

Dumas, G. (1948). *La vie affective.* Paris: Presses Universitaires de France.

Eibl-Eibesfeldt, I. (1972). Similarities and differences between cultures in expressive movements. In R. A. Hinde (Ed.), *Nonverbal communication* (pp. 297-311). Cambridge, MA: Cambridge University Press.

Ekman, P., Friesen, W. V., & Ellsworth, P. C. (1972). *Emotion in the human face: Guidelines for research and an integration of findings.* New York: Pergamon Press.

Ekman, P., Levenson, R. W., & Friesen, W. V. (1983). Autonomic nervous system activity distinguishes among emotions. *Science, 221*(4616), 1208-1210.

Ekman, P., Sorenson, E. R., & Friesen, W. V. (1969). Pancultural elements in facial displays of emotions. *Science, 164*(3875), 86-88.

Emde, R., Katz, E., & Thorpe, J. (1978). Emotional expression in infancy: II. Early deviations in Down's syndrome. In M. Lewis & L. Rosenblum (Eds.), *The development of affect.* New York: Plenum Press.

Eysenck, H. J. (1952). *The scientific study of personality.* London: Rouledge and Kegan Paul.

Flynn, J. P. (1967). The neural basis of aggression in cats. In D. C. Glass (Ed.), *Neurophysiology and emotion.* New York: Rockefeller University Press.

Forgas, J. P., & Bower, G. H. (1987). Mood effects on person-perception judgments. *Journal of Personality and Social Psychology, 53*(1), 53-60.

Fox, N. A., & Davidson, R. J. (1984). Hemispheric substrates of affect: A developmental model. In N. A. Fox & R. J. Davidson (Eds.), *The psychobiology of affective development* (pp. 353-381). Hillsdale, NJ: Erlbaum.

Fridlund, A. J., Schwartz, G. E., & Fowler, S. C. (1984). Pattern recognition of self-reported emotional state from multiple-site facial EMG activity during affective imagery. *Psychophysiology, 21*(6), 622-637.

Goldsmith, H., Buss, A., Plomin, R., Rothbart, M., Thomas, A., Chess, S., Hinde, R., & McCall, R. (1987). Roundtable: What is temperament? Four approaches. *Child Development, 58,* 505-529.

Goldsmith, H. H., & Campos, J. J. (1982). Toward a theory of infant temperament. In R. Emde & R. J. Harmon (Eds.), *The development of attachment and affiliative systems.* New York: Plenum Press.

Gray, J. A. (1982). Precis of the neuropsychology of anxiety: An inquiry into the functions of the septo-hippocampal system. *Behavioral and Brain Sciences, 5,* 469-534.

Greenspan, S. I., & Porges, S. W. (1985). Psychopathology in infancy and early childhood: Clinical perspectives on the organization of sensory and affective-thematic experience. *Child Development, 55,* 49-70.

Haviland, J. M., & Lelwica, M. (1987). The induced affect response: 10-week-old infants' responses to three emotion expressions. *Developmental Psychology, 23*(1), 97-104.

Hoffman, M. L. (1978). Empathy, its development and prosocial implications. In C. B. Keasey (Ed.), *Nebraska symposium on motivation* (Vol. 25) (pp. 169-218). Lincoln, NE: University of Nebraska Press.

Hoffman, M. L. (1985). Affect, motivation, and cognition. In E. T. Higgins & R. M. Sorrentino (Eds.), *Handbook of motivation and cognition: Foundations of social behavior* (pp. 244-280). New York: Guilford.

Hu, J. W., Dostrovsky, J. O., & Sessle, B. J. (1981). Functional properties of neurons in cat trigeminal subnucleus caudalis (medullary dorsal horn). I. Responses to oral-facial noxious and nonnoxious stimuli and

projections to thalamus and subnucleus oralis. *Journal of Neurophysiology, 45*(2), 173-192.
Huebner, R. R., & Izard, C. E. (1988). Mothers' responses to infants' facial expressions of sadness, anger, and physical distress. *Motivation and Emotion, 12*(2), 185-196.
Hyson, M. C., & Izard, C. E. (1985). Continuities and changes in emotion expressions during brief separation at 13 and 18 months. *Developmental Psychology, 24*(6), 1165-1170.
Isen, A. (1984). Toward understanding the role of affect in cognition. In R. Wyer & T. Srull (Eds.), *Handbook of social cognition* (pp. 179-236). Hillsdale, NJ: Erlbaum.
Isen, A. M., & Daubman, K. A. (1984). The influence of affect on categorization. *Journal of Personality and Social Psychology, 47,* 1206-1217.
Isen, A. M., Daubman, K.A., & Norwicki, G. P. (1987). Positive affect facilitates creative problem solving. *Journal of Personality and Social Psychology, 52*(6), 1122-1131.
Isen, A. M., Shalker, T. E., Clark, M., & Karp, L. (1978). Affect, accessibility of material in memory and behavior: A cognitive loop? *Journal of Personality and Social Psychology, 36,* 1-12.
Izard, C. E. (1968). *The emotions as a culture-common framework of motivational experiences and communicative cues.* [Technical Report No. 30, Contract No. NR2149(33)]. Washington, D.C.: Office of Naval Research, 316-317.
Izard, C. E. (1971). *The face of emotion.* New York: Appleton-Century-Crofts.
Izard, C. E. (1977). *Human emotions.* New York: Plenum Press.
Izard, C. E. (1979). *The maximally discriminative facial movement coding system (Max).* Newark, DE: University of Delaware, ACIT - Instructional Technology.
Izard, C. E. (1988). *Facial expressions and the regulation of emotions.* Manuscript submitted for publication.
Izard, C. E., Hembree, E. A., Dougherty, L. M., & Spizzirri, C. C. (1983). Changes in facial expressions of 2- to 19-month-old infants following acute pain. *Developmental Psychology, 19*(3), 418-426.
Izard, C. E., Hembree, E. A., & Huebner, R. R. (1987). Infants' emotion expressions to acute pain: Developmental change and stability of individual differences. *Developmental Psychology, 23*(1), 105-113.
Izard, C. E., Huebner, R. R., Risser, D., McGinnes, G., & Dougherty, L. (1980). The young infant's ability to reproduce discrete emotion expressions. *Development Psychology, 16*(2), 132-140.
Izard, C. E., & Malatesta, C. Z. (1987). Perspectives on emotional development: I. Differential emotions theory of early emotional development. In J. D. Osofsky (Ed.), *Handbook of infant development* (2nd ed.) (pp. 494-554). New York: Wiley-Interscience.
Izard, C. E., & Schwartz, G. M. (1986). Patterns of emotion in depression. In M. Rutter, C. E. Izard, & P. B. Read (Eds.), *Depression in young people: Developmental and clinical perspectives.* New York: Guilford Press.
Izard, C. E., Wehmer, G. M., Livsey, W., & Jennings, J. R. (1965). Affect, awareness, and performance. In S. S. Tomkins & C. E. Izard (Eds.), *Affect, cognition, and personality* (pp. 2-41). New York: Springer.
James, W. (1884). What is emotion? *Mind, 4,* 188-204.

Kagan, J. (1984). The idea of emotion in human development. In C. E. Izard, J. Kagan, & R. Zajonc (Eds.), *Emotions, cognition, and behavior* (pp. 38-72). New York: Cambridge University Press.
Kagan, J., & Moss, H. (1962). *A birth to maturity*. New York: Wiley.
Kagan, J., Reznick, J. S., & Snidman, N. (1988). Biological bases of childhood shyness. *Science, 240,* 167-171.
Kihlstrom, J. F. (1987). The cognitive unconscious. *Science, 237,* 1445-1452.
Klinnert, M., Campos, J. J., Sorce, J., Emde, R., & Svejda, M. (1983). Emotions as behavior regulators: The development of social referencing. In R. Plutchik & H. Kellerman (Eds.), *Emotions in early development: Vol 2. Emotion: Theory, research and experience* (pp. 57-86). New York: Academic Press.
Laird, J. D. (1984). Facial response and emotion. *Journal of Personality and Social Psychology, 47,* 909-917.
Lang, P. J. (1984). Cognition in emotion: Concept and action. In C. E. Izard, J. Kagan, & R. B. Zajonc (Eds.), *Emotions, cognition, and behavior* (pp. 192-226). New York: Cambridge University Press.
Langsdorf, P., Izard, C. E., Rayias, M., & Hembree, E. (1983). Interest expression, visual fixation, and heart rate changes in 2- to 8-month old infants. *Developmental Psychology, 19*(3), 375-386.
Lanzetta, J. T., Cartwright-Smith, J. E., & Kleck, R. E. (1976). Effects of nonverbal dissimulation of emotional experience and autonomic arousal. *Journal of Personality and Social Psychology, 33,* 354-370.
Lazarus, R. S. (1984). On the primacy of cognition. *American Psychologist, 39*(2), 124-129.
Lazarus, R. S., Kanner, A. D., & Folkman, S. (1980). Emotions: A cognitive phenomenological analysis. In R. Plutchik & H. Kellerman (Eds.), *Emotion: Theory, research, and experience: Vol. 1. Theories of emotion* (pp. 189-217). New York: Academic Press.
LeDoux, J. E. (1987). Emotion. In F. Plum (Ed.), *Handbook of physiology—The nervous system* (Section 1, Vol. V) (pp. 419-459). Washington, D. C.: American Physiological Society.
LeDoux, J. E. (1986). Neurobiology of emotion. In J. E. LeDoux & W. Hirst (Eds.), *Mind and brain* (pp. 301-354). New York: Cambridge University Press.
Leeper, R. W. (1948). A motivational theory of emotion to replace "emotion as disorganized response." *Psychological Review, 55,* 5-21.
Lewis, M., & Michalson, L. (1983). *Children's emotions and moods: Developmental theory and measurement.* New York: Plenum Press.
Main, M., Tomasini, L., & Tolan, W. (1979). Differences among mothers of infants judged to differ in security. *Developmental Psychology, 15,* 472-473.
Malatesta, C. Z., & Haviland, J. M. (1982). Learning display rules: The socialization of emotion expression in infancy. *Child Development, 53,* 991-1003.
Matsumoto, D. (1987). The role of facial response in the experience of emotion: More methodological problems and a meta-analysis. *Journal of Personality and Social Psychology, 52*(4), 769-774.
Mineka, S., Davidson, M., Cook, M., & Keir, R. (1984). Observational conditioning of snake fear in rhesus monkeys. *Journal of Abnormal Psychology, 93*(4), 355-372.

Mowrer, O. H. (1960). *Learning theory and behavior.* New York: Wiley.
Nasby, W., & Yando, R. (1982). Selective encoding and retrieval of affectively valent information: Two cognitive consequences of children's mood states. *Journal of Personality and Social Psychology, 43*(6), 1244-1253.
Oster, H. (1978). Facial expression and affect development, In L. Lewis & L. Rosenblum (Eds.), *The development of affect.* New York: Plenum Press.
Plutchik, R. (1980). A general psychoevolutionary theory of emotion. In R. Plutchik & H. Kellerman (Eds.). *Emotion: Theory, research, and experience.* (Vol. 1). New York: Academic Press.
Rinn, W. E. (1984). The neuropsychology of facial expression: A review of the neurological and psychological mechanisms for producing facial expressions. *Psychological Bulletin, 95*(1), 52-77.
Rothbart, M. K., & Derryberry, D. (1981). Development of individual differences in temperament. In M. E. Lamb & A. L. Brown (Eds.) *Advances in developmental psychology* (Vol. 1) (pp. 37-86). Hillsdale, NJ: Erlbaum.
Rusalova, M. N., Izard, C. E., & Simonov, P. V. (1975). Comparative analysis of mimical and autonomic components of man's emotional state. *Aviation, Space, and Environmental Medicine, 46*(9), 1132-1134.
Sagi, A., & Hoffman, M. L. (1976). Empathic distress in the newborn. *Developmental Psychology, 12*(2), 175-176.
Scarr, S., & Salapatek P. (1970). Patterns of fear development during infancy. *Merrill-Palmer Quarterly, 16,* 53-90.
Schwartz, G. E. (1982). Psychophysiological patterning and emotion revisited: A systems perspective. In C. E. Izard (Ed.), *Measuring emotions in infants and children* (pp. 67-93). New York: Cambridge University Press.
Schwartz, G. E., Weinberger, D. A., & Singer, J. A. (1981). Cardiovascular differentiation of happiness, sadness, anger, and fear following imagery and exercise. *Psychosomatic Medicine, 43,* 343-364.
Sirota, A. D., Schwartz, G. E., & Kristeller, J. L. (1987). Facial muscle activity during induced mood states: Differential growth and carryover of elated versus depressed patterns. *Psychophysiology, 24,* 691-699.
Sperry, R. (1982). Some effects of disconnecting the cerebral hemispheres. *Science, 217,* 1223-1226.
Termine, N. T., & Izard, C. E. (1988). Infants' responses to their mothers' expressions of joy and sadness. *Developmental Psychology, 24*(2), 223-229.
Thomas, A., & Chess, S. (1977). *Temperament and development.* New York: Brunner/Mazel.
Tomkins, S. S. (1962). *Affect, imagery, consciousness: Vol. 1. The positive affects.* New York: Springer.
Tomkins, S. S. (1963). *Affect, imagery, consciousness: Vol. 2. The negative affects.* New York: Springer.
Tronick, E., Ricks, M., & Cohn, J. (1982). Maternal and infant affective exchange: Patterns of adaptation. In T. Field & A. Fogel (Eds.), *Emotion and early interaction.* Hillsdale, NJ: Erlbaum.
Washburn, R. W. (1929). A study of the smiling and laughing of infants in the first year of life. *Genetic Psychology Monographs, 6*(5), 397-535.
Watson, D. (1988). Intraindividual and interindividual analyses of positive and negative affect: Their relation to health complaints, perceived stress, and daily activities. *Journal of Personality and Social Psychology, 54*(6), 1020-1030.

Watson, D., & Tellegen, A. (1985). Toward a consensual structure of mood. *Psychological Bulletin, 98,* 219-235.

Weiner, B., & Graham, S. (1984). An attributional approach to emotional development. In C. E. Izard, J. Kagan, & R. Zajonc (Eds.), *Emotions, cognition, & behavior.* New York: Cambridge University Press.

Weisenfeld, A. R., & Klorman, R. (1978). The mother's psychophysiological reactions to contrasting affective expressions by her own and an unfamiliar infant. *Developmental Psychology, 14*(3), 294-304.

Winton, W. M. (1986). The role of facial response in self-reports of emotions: A critique of Laird. *Journal of Personality and Social Psychology, 50,* 808-812.

Wolff, P. H. (1969). The natural history of crying and other vocalizations in early infancy. In B. M. Foss (Ed.), *Determinants of infant behavior* (pp. 81-109). London: Methuen.

Zahn-Waxler, C., Radke-Yarrow, M., & King, R. A. (1979). Child rearing and children's prosocial initiations towards victims of distress. *Child Development, 50,* 319-330.

Zajonc, R. B. (1980). Feeling and thinking: Preferences need no inferences. *American Psychologist, 35*(2), 151-175.

Zajonc, R. B. (1984). On the primacy of affect. *American Psychologist, 39,* 117-123.

MARTIN E. P. SELIGMAN

RESEARCH IN CLINICAL PSYCHOLOGY: WHY IS THERE SO MUCH DEPRESSION TODAY?

Martin E. P. Seligman is professor of psychology and director of clinical training at the University of Pennsylvania, where he has been a faculty member since 1972. He has an AB degree from Princeton University, a PhD degree from the University of Pennsylvania, and a PhD *Honoris causa* from Uppsala University, Sweden.

Seligman has authored or coauthored more than 100 articles and 5 books, including *Abnormal Psychology* (1984, with Rosenhan), *Human Helplessness: Theory and Application* (1980, edited with Garber), *Psychopathology Experimental Models* (1977, edited with Maser), and *Helplessness: On Depression, Development, and Death* (1975). His professional activities include serving as Chairman of the Scientific Board for Foresight, Inc.; on the Advisory Council of the National Institute for the Clinical Application of Behavioral Medicine; as Advisor for *Psychology Today*; and as Principal Investigator for the National Institute of Mental Health on helplessness and attributional style in children, and for the National Institute on Aging on explanatory style as a predictor of mortality and morbidity. He is also a Fellow of the American Psychological Association (Experimental, Comparative, Clinical, Aging, and Health Divisions), the American Association for the Advancement of Science, the Behaviour Research and Therapy Society, and the Society of Behavioral Medicine.

MARTIN E. P. SELIGMAN

RESEARCH IN CLINICAL PSYCHOLOGY: WHY IS THERE SO MUCH DEPRESSION TODAY?

Depression has been strongly on the rise since World War II. Two large-scale epidemiological studies have suggested that young people now have about 10 times more risk for unipolar depression than their grandparents had. The Amish have about the same rate of bipolar depression as contemporary non-Amish Americans but have a much lower rate of unipolar depression. This suggests that something about modern life provides fertile soil for unipolar depression. What?

I see unipolar depression as primarily a disorder in which individual goals are thwarted (learned helplessness). We live in an age of growing individualism and of shrinking commitment to larger societal institutions, or the *commons*. Two developments have contributed to the growth of individualism: machine intelligence that has created a profitable market for customized taste and individual purchasing power that has increased substantially in modern times. At the same time, the decline of religion, the family, and commitment to the nation has weakened the buffering effect of faith in the commons against depression. This has left the individual with little to fall back

This work was supported in part by National Institute of Mental Health (NIMH) Grant 19604, NIMH Grant 41402, National Institute on Aging Grant AGO5590, and by a grant from the MacArthur Foundation Research Network on Determinants and Consequences of Health-Promoting and Health-Damaging Behavior.

on when he or she fails personally. Under these conditions, individual helplessness may prove to be more depressing than it has in the past. Although individualism may bring depression in its wake and may make it more difficult to find meaning, it should not be surrendered lightly.

Individualism and Depression

The story that follows is told primarily for the benefit of teachers of undergraduates. I have chosen the most startling new findings in the field of depression, findings that seem, nevertheless, to have been neglected in the press and in textbooks. As you will see, I believe that these findings have sweeping societal implications and, at the same time, have immediacy for undergraduate students. The story comes in three parts.

First, I will argue that there is, literally, an epidemic of depression today. Something has happened in America, roughly since World War II, so that depression is about 10 times as common as it used to be. Four independent lines of evidence suggest that this is so. I will detail two well-conducted, large-scale studies showing that the lifetime prevalence of depression in young people now exceeds by roughly a factor of 10 its prevalence in young people 50 years ago. I will then look at two contemporary societies of people who do not live in modern culture—the Kaluli of New Guinea and the old order Amish of Lancaster County, Pennsylvania. Neither of these premodern cultures has depression at anything like the prevalence found in modern cultures.

When we put this together, we see that something about modern life seems to create fertile soil for depression. In the second part of the story, we will ask, What?

I will suggest that four sets of singular, historical facts have changed the economic, political, and institutional situations in the West. Of these, two sets of facts have exalted the self and two others have weakened the buffering effect of the larger institutions that I call the *commons*. I will suggest that depression is a disorder of the individual, particularly of learned helplessness when the self is thwarted. Taken together, this results in individuals, preoccupied with their own hedonics, who take the ordinary failures of life badly and have few larger beliefs to fall back on for consolation.

Finally, I will speculate on the implications of the epidemic of depression for the future of individualism and for the psychology of personal control, and I will end by suggesting that hope lies in striking a healthier balance between commitment to the self and commitment to the common good.

Is This an Age of Melancholy?

Gerald Klerman first coined the apt term, "the age of melancholy" (Klerman, 1979), to describe modern times in the West. He did so in the course of sponsoring two major epidemiological studies while he was director of the Alcohol, Drug Abuse, and Mental Health Administration. Both of these epidemiological studies suggest a tenfold difference in the rate of depression over the last two generations. Both studies, though the best of their kind ever conducted, are imperfect. But when they are taken together, they point to what looks like an important fact.

In the Epidemiological Catchment Area (ECA) study, over 9,500 people were given the same structured diagnostic interview from 1980 to 1982. Rates of *DSM-III* disorders were obtained (Myers et al., 1984; Robins et al., 1984). This standard interview, given to people of different ages, answers the important question, Is the instance of depression different for people who are born in different times?

The second epidemiological study was a parallel study but used subjects who were close relatives of people with major depressive disorder rather than a large representative random sample (Klerman et al., 1985). This study also had a sample size large enough to yield results that answered the question, Depending on what year you were born in, do you have a different risk of depressive disorder?

Let us now turn to the details of these two studies.

The ECA Study

In the ECA study (Myers et al., 1984; Robins et al., 1984), the National Institute of Mental Health decided that it was going to spend a great deal of money to answer these questions definitively: What is the prevalence of depression in America? Are there male/female differences? Are there age differences? They did this for most other forms of psychopathology as well. The knowledge of these rates allows the rational planning of future therapeutic resources. For those of you who teach or are students of psychiatric epidemiology, this is a landmark study. We now know with considerable certainty the rates of different disorders in America. But what is going to interest us most is a remarkable fact about depression that surprised all of the researchers.

Let me say something about how the study was conducted. Roughly 9,500 adults were randomly and representatively sampled. There were six data collection centers, both rural and urban. Only the urban data have been published, and they came from three cities: Baltimore, New Haven, and St. Louis.

What I am going to focus on is the lifetime prevalence of a major depressive disorder and on how this prevalence changes with present age and decade of birth. The *lifetime prevalence* of a disorder is defined as the percentage of the population that has had the disorder at least once in their lifetime. This is a cumulative statistic, so the older the individual, everything else being equal, the higher the chance that he or she will have had the disorder. If you look at the lifetime prevalence of broken legs, you will find that it goes up with age, since those who are older have had more opportunities to break a leg. What everyone expected was that those born earlier in the century would have a higher lifetime prevalence for depressive disorder because they would have had more years to experience it; for example, a person born in 1920 has had 30 more years to possibly experience depression than someone born in 1950.

The occurrence of major depressive disorder was well-defined. It was ascertained by describing each symptom of depression systematically and asking each member of the sample if he or she experienced the symptom at any time in his or her life. These symptoms include prolonged low mood, suicidal thoughts and action, low self-esteem, loss of interest in usually enjoyable activities, lack of motivation, and appetite loss.

Table 1
Lifetime Prevalence of Major Depressive Episode by Age

	18-24 yrs born c. 1960 n=1397	25-44 yrs c. 1945 n=3722	45-64 yrs c.1925 n=2351	over 65 c. 1910 n=1654
New Haven %	7.5	10.4	4.2	1.8
Baltimore %	4.1	7.5	4.2	1.4
St. Louis %	4.5	8.0	5.2	0.8

Note. Adapted from Robins et al. (1984) by permission. Copyright 1984–85, American Medical Association.

As Table 1 shows, if you were born around 1960, that is, if you were about 20–25 years old at the time of the interview, your probability of having had at least one episode of major depressive disorder would be 5% or 6%. If you were 25–44 years old, your risk would go up to about 8% or 9%, as any sensible cumulative statistic should. And now something odd seems to happen.

Even though you would have had much more opportunity to contract the disorder, the rate would plummet to little more than 4% if you were born around 1925. Finally, your grandparents, born around World War I, would have a rate of only about 1%, in spite of

70 years of opportunity to have had major depressive disorder. That is a very puzzling finding.

It is hard to resist hunting for flaws and artifacts in these data. The major flaw is that the data are retrospective: They emerge from self-reports of depression after the fact, sometimes long after the fact. Another flaw is that the data divide people into cases or not cases of depressive disorder. They do not tell us about the whole continuum from mild to severe depression but only about the prevalence of severe depression. In addition, there are several possible artifacts, which are all pointed to by the fact that most disorders show a trend in this puzzling direction. Schizophrenia, for example, has about twice the lifetime prevalence for the two youngest cohorts as for the two oldest cohorts. But no other disorder shows the huge reverse trend that depression does.

Differential survival is one possible artifact: Those who were included in this sample had to have made it to the interview, that is, they had to be alive and not in jail or in the hospital. Perhaps many of the depressives had died off or were otherwise eliminated, leaving an inflated number of nondepressed survivors in the oldest groups. Since there are probably higher rates of mortality, certainly by suicide and even by illness, in depression-prone people, this is not implausible (Peterson, Seligman, & Vaillant, 1988). The problem with this account is the sheer size of the difference in incidence. A tenfold difference in depression cannot be accounted for by a presumably much smaller difference in selective mortality and illness.

Differential memory is a more plausible artifact. On this account, people forget that they had suicidal thoughts or chronic blues. The farther in time they are from when they had these symptoms, the more they forget. If depression tends to occur when people are young, then old people are farther in time away from these symptoms and so are more likely to forget them. In reply to this, when these people were asked to report their depressive symptoms in the last 6 months (which holds the forgetting interval constant), the young group still reported about 5 times as much depression as the oldest group (Myers et al., 1984). But again, although this artifact is somewhat plausible, it is unlikely to account for a tenfold difference.

The differential willingness to report symptoms is also plausible. Perhaps older people are more reluctant to admit to unpleasant symptoms. Remember, however, that the difference is larger for depression than for other disorders, so it is sadness and similar feelings rather than hallucinations or drinking that older people particularly avoid reporting. This explanation is also plausible but also unlikely to account for the difference by disorder and is very unlikely to account for a tenfold difference in depression.

So the finding of more depression in people born later in this century is probably not an artifact of survival, of reporting, or of memory. I lean strongly toward the possibility that people born later in this century have actually experienced much more depression than those born earlier.

The Relatives Study

Let us now turn to the second epidemiological study (Klerman et al., 1985). It is similar in design and in scale to the first study. The difference is the sample. First, 523 people were diagnosed as having major affective disorder. They had 2,289 first-degree relatives—fathers, mothers, brothers, sisters, sons, and daughters—who all received the same structured diagnostic interview to determine their risk for major depressive disorder. The size of the sample was large enough to enable the researchers to answer the same question of risk with birth cohort that the ECA sample asked.

Again, Figure 1 shows a ten-to-one effect. Consider just the data for the females (the males show basically the same effect, only with half the absolute rate of depression). What the complicated curves show is the following: Consider just people who were born before 1910, the generation of your grandmothers or great grandmothers. As you can see, by the time the respondents in your grandmothers' generation had reached age 20, only 1% or 2% of those who later

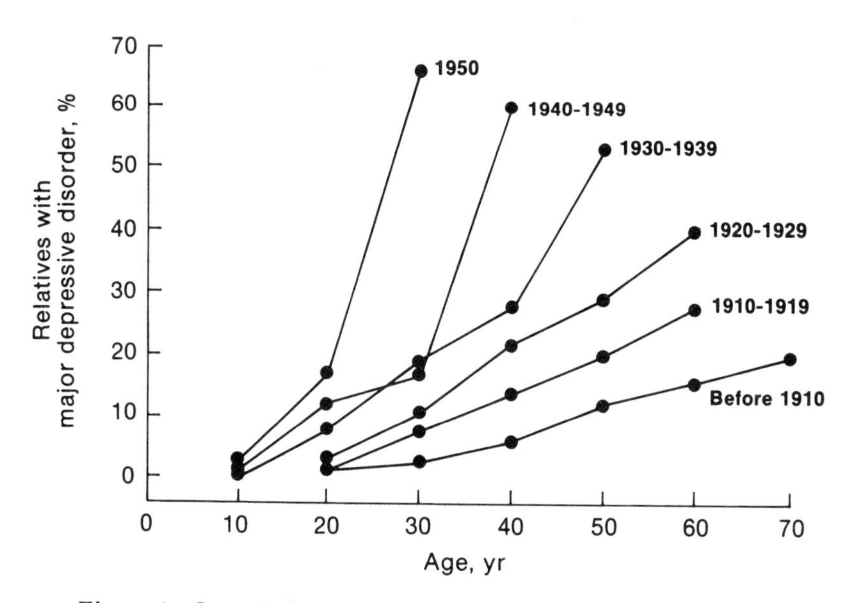

Figure 1. Cumulative probability of diagnosable major depressive disorder in female relatives by birth cohort. From Klerman et al. (1985) with permission. Copyright 1984–85, American Medical Association.

had a depressed relative had themselves had a depressive disorder. By the time they had reached age 70, perhaps 10%–15% had had a depressive disorder. That is a much larger prevalence than the ECA sample because, of course, these women were at a genetic risk for depression. Now, look at the 1950 birth year curve, from age 20 and age 30. These data imply that, if you are 30 years old and you were born around 1950, your risk for depressive disorders is about 60%, whereas your great grandmother's risk for depression was about 3% by the time she reached 30. Figures 2 and 3 use rigorous statistical methods to document this phenomenon (Reich et al., 1987).

Figure 2 is the survival distribution, the percentage of people who will remain depression-free after a given age. In this figure, they are divided into three age groups: people over 45, people between 25 and 45, and people under 25. In the survival function of those older than 45 years, about 20% of the females with first-degree depressed relatives will get depressed by the time they die. Among those younger than 25 years, about 30% have already become depressed.

Figure 3 suggests that an earlier age of the first depression episode is one operative factor here (Reich et al., 1987). Depression not only has been getting more frequent in modern times but also has been occurring much earlier in life the first time. So for those born in 1938, the mean age range for first depression would have been from 30 to 35 years. For those born in 1956, first depression would have occurred, on average, between the ages of 20 and 25 years.

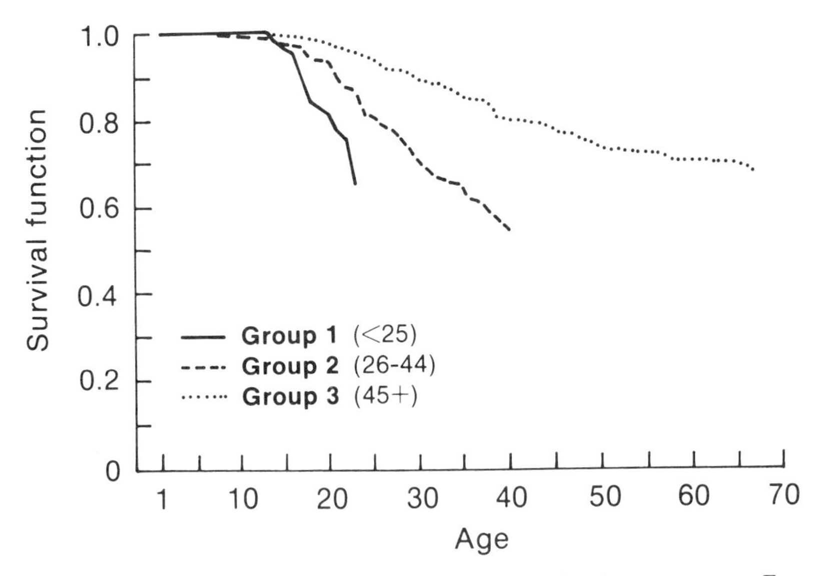

Figure 2. Female survival distribution stratified by age group. From Reich et al. (1987) with permission. Copyright 1987, Pergamon Press plc.

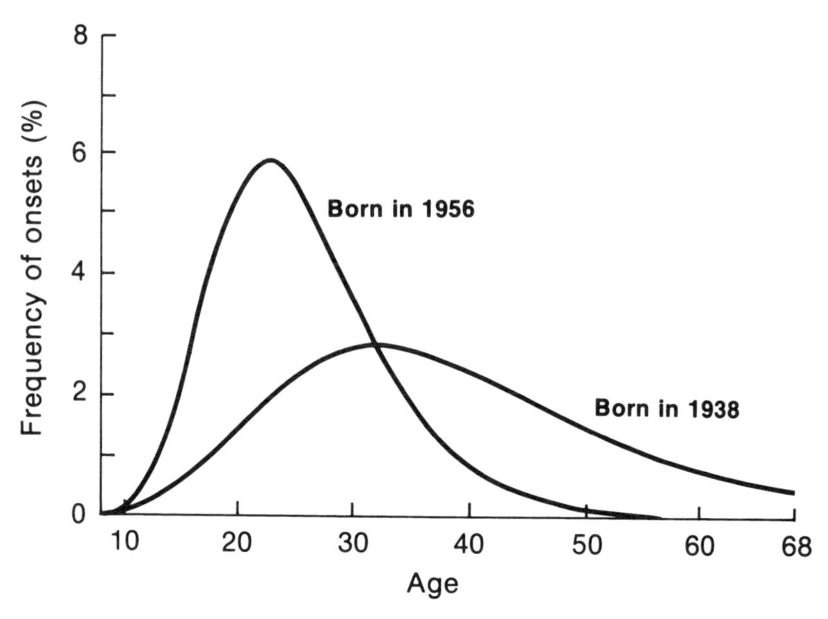

Figure 3. Age of onset distribution of primary major depressive disorder in two birth cohorts. From Reich et al. (1987) with permission. Copyright 1987, Pergamon Press plc.

One dissenting note before I go on: The authors of these studies interpreted them as showing a "gene-environment interaction" (Klerman, 1988; Klerman et al., 1985), in keeping with their biomedical orientation. I see no evidence in these data supporting a gene-environment interaction. On the contrary, it looks like the risk of depression both for genetically vulnerable people and for people in the general population has increased about tenfold. This is not an interaction over time; rather, it points to a purely environmental effect.

The second study is subject to the same possible artifacts as the first. It will not be easy to test the extent to which these artifacts produce the tenfold difference, or at least part of it. In the meantime, I take the straightforward interpretation and assume that people experience much more depression now than they did two generations ago. Why?

The Kaluli and the Amish: Contemporary Cultures With Little Depression

Something about modernity has brought about this vulnerability to depression. Looking at just the first two studies, we see that any historical factor that coincides with recent times might be responsible for the increase. Global warming, nuclear fallout, or increased nationalism, for example, cannot be ruled out. The next two studies implicate modern Western culture.

For years, people have looked anecdotally at the incidence of depression in non-Western cultures. On the whole, you do not find much in the way of depression as we know it—suicide, hopelessness, giving up, low self-esteem, passivity, and the like—in non-Western cultures before they are modernized. Typically, when depression appears, as it does occasionally in China, it has somatic rather than mood and cognitive symptoms (e.g., Kleinman, 1982). In fact, investigators seem to be straining to call this disorder depression. When you look at even more primitive and less Westernized cultures, you may not see any depression.

There is a primitive tribe in New Guinea called the Kaluli. Sheiffelin (1984) tried to find the equivalent of depression among them. Briefly, the Kaluli do not seem to have despair, hopelessness, depression, or suicide in the way that we know them. What they do have is quite interesting. If a tribe member loses something valuable, such as a pig, he has a right to recompense. There are rituals (such as dancing and screaming at the neighbor who might have killed the pig) recognized by the society. When the victim demands recompense for loss, either the neighbor or the whole tribe takes note of the loss and usually recompenses the victim in one way or another. The point I want to make here is that reciprocity between the culture and the individual when loss occurs buffers the individual and thus prevents the loss from becoming prolonged helplessness and hopelessness. I want to suggest that a society that prevents loss from becoming hopelessness and prevents sadness from becoming despair, in so doing, breaks up the process of depression. Societies that promote, as ours does, the transition from loss to helplessness to hopelessness also promote depression. I will return to this hypothesis when I discuss the elements of modern life that produce despair.

We do not need to look at stone-age tribes to see societies with low rates of depression. There is one in our own backyard. Janice Egeland has, for the last 20 years, led a monumental study of the mental health of the old order Amish of Pennsylvania (Egeland & Hostetter, 1983; Egeland, Hostetter, & Eshleman, 1983). There are 10,000 old order Amish living in Lancaster County, Pennsylvania. The Amish are a premodern culture. They stem from four families that emigrated to the United States in about 1750; they were pacifists trying to escape the draft in Germany. The old order Amish form a farming culture that uses no electricity. There are no automobiles. There is no use of alcohol or drugs. The culture is mid-nineteenth century in all forms, and it is a very tight-knit community. There is no inward migration; there is some outward migration. This culture is a boon for studying the genetics of bipolar depression, and that is mostly what Egeland has studied. But it is not our main interest.

Egeland developed a network within the community for reporting potential disorders and then used diagnostic interviews to confirm the presence and kind of disorder. Given the rigor with which Egeland's group made diagnoses, it is fair to compare the Amish with the sample in the ECA study of Baltimoreans, a mere hundred miles away.

The Amish have about the same lifetime prevalence of bipolar depression and manic depressive disorder as the people in Baltimore—1% or 2%. But I wish to emphasize that that percentage is also roughly the rate of unipolar depression among the Amish. That is, depression without mania, common cold depression, occurs at roughly one fifth to one tenth the rate among the Amish as it does among people in Baltimore.

As further evidence, a major study of a rural county in eastern Canada should be mentioned (Murphy, Sobol, Neff, Olivier, & Leighton, 1984). The prevalence of depression was measured in 1952 and again in 1970. Rates of depression seemed low and stable, and there was no sign of an increase in depression among younger people across time. (Caution is in order because Murphy et al.'s technique of measuring depression does not map exactly onto the prior epidemiological studies.) It seems important that this was a stable, rural society that had not dramatically changed over the last three decades.

These then are the five lines of evidence that suggest that modernity has produced a huge increase in vulnerability to unipolar depression. To review: Two large-sample studies seem to show that there has been a tenfold increase in the risk for depression for people born in the last 30 years versus those born 70 years ago. I suggest that this has to do with modernity because contemporary nonmodern cultures, such as the Amish, seem to have unipolar depression not at our rate, but at roughly the rate of our culture two generations ago. The rest of this paper assumes that the rise in depression has occurred in fact and not in artifact.

Modernity and Depression

What has happened since World War II in the West that makes your young students and your young patients so much more vulnerable to depression than were their parents and grandparents? I want to approach this question by musing not about the world but about psychology itself.

A Sea Change in Psychology

When I was a graduate student in psychology, almost 25 years ago, human action was explained in a very different way from the way human action is explained now. What then counted as an explanation for human action was that people were pushed or pulled by their environment. The details of this pushing and pulling depended on the specific theory, but in outline all fashionable theories were push–pull.

Here are some paraphrases of theories that will sound familiar to you:

1. Organisms persist in their responses if their responses are reinforced by positive events or the offset of negative events.
2. Organisms display their habits when their biological drives are high and will repeat those responses that have been followed by tissue need reduction.
3. Under appropriate releasing conditions, animals display fixed action patterns.
4. Adult behavior is driven by unresolved sexual and aggressive conflicts from childhood.
5. When organisms are frustrated, aggression results.

In all of these theories, people act because they are driven from within or without. But it now seems obvious to us that, at least some of the time, people choose their own course of action. They decide, prefer, plan, and choose. However, in the 1950s and early 1960s, such explanations were not just unfashionable, they were forbidden.

Starting around 1965, what counted as an explanation in psychology underwent a sea change. Here are the sorts of explanations we now teach our students:

1. When individuals expect that nothing that they do matters, they will become helpless and will not initiate action.
2. Successful action flows from a sense of self-efficacy.
3. Individuals plan and monitor their own actions, reinforce themselves, and correct their unsuccessful actions.
4. Individuals decide from among expected outcomes and choose the most highly preferred.

The site of action has changed from outside the self to within the self. Individual expectations, choice, decision, and hedonics are literally where the action now is. I am going to suggest that this sea change in explanation is intimately related to an exaltation (dare I say reification) of the individual over the last 25 years in society at large. And then I am going to argue that the exaltation of the individual creates fertile ground for a rise in depression.

When do sea changes in scientific explanation occur? Sociologists of science contend that new explanations in science come about (are legitimized) when larger historical forces act on the society at large. Consider a highly relevant past case: Francis Bacon and the rise of modern science.

Until the Renaissance, Western science was concerned almost exclusively with the prediction and description of nature. At the end of the Middle Ages, Francis Bacon (1561–1626) made the radical suggestion that science need not be confined to description and prediction. He suggested that scientists could conduct experiments, that scientists could actually manipulate nature. From Bacon's suggestion, Western science became an endeavor with the additional aim of controlling natural forces. Human beings came to believe, apparently for the first time, that they could control nature.

What might have occurred in Bacon's time to legitimize the notion that people could control nature? One speculation is the ending of feudalism. Bacon's father, Sir Nicholas Bacon (1509–1579), was the first person in centuries from Bacon's previously humble family to move up dramatically in society. In 1618, Bacon himself rose to the office of lord chancellor of England. What had happened to Bacon's family in the previous century mirrored a much wider change in the social fabric of Europe. In the prior two centuries, the Black Death had swept Europe, killing as many as one third of the adults in a short time. New jobs were open to peasants for the first time since feudalism began, and with revolutionary fervor, the peasants seized them. I suggest that people came to believe that if something as fixed as the social order could change, perhaps the natural order could be changed as well.

Returning to the change in the social sciences from focusing on the environment to focusing on the individual, what might have happened in our lifetime to legitimize it?

The Age of the Individual

During the first term of his presidency, Ronald Reagan gave a speech on Wall Street entitled "The Age of the Individual." I believe that Mr. Reagan was exactly right: We live, for the first time in Western history, in an age of personal control. I want to suggest that there are (at least) four historical themes that have converged to make this the age of the individual. The first two have exalted the self. The last two have weakened the buffering commitment of the exalted self to larger institutions. And one untoward consequence of this convergence is a massive increase in depression.

The rhinestone refrigerator. When the assembly line was created at the turn of this century, its governing idea was that it would be more profitable to paint every refrigerator white, that is, more profitable to produce a standardized product. In the 1950s, with the development of the transistor and rudimentary machine intelligence, it became just as profitable to encrust every hundredth refrigerator with rhinestones. Machine intelligence opened an enormous market for customization, for individual choice. Now blue jeans are no longer all blue; they come in hundreds of varieties and dozens of colors. There are probably a thousand models of cars and almost as many kinds of beer. Even Mao jackets can be tailored to individual caprice. To tap this market, advertising exalted individual choice. The deciding, choosing, hedonically preoccupied individual became a profitable institution. The exalted individual became a new reality for social science to explain. Furthermore, when the individual has a lot of money to spend, individualism becomes a powerful and profitable worldview.

General prosperity. America is a Croesus-rich country. I am not going to enter the debate about the groups that have been left out of this prosperity. The fact is that, on the average, Americans now have more buying power than ever before in history. Wealth today means something different than it did in centuries past. Consider the medieval prince, wealthy, but most of what he owned was literally inalienable. He could no more sell his land and go out and buy horses than he could sell his title. His wealth, unlike ours, was not purchasing power. Our wealth, in contrast, is tied to the bewildering array of choices opened to us by the rhinestone refrigerator. We have more records, more clothes, more education, more concerts and books, more knowledge, some even say more love to choose from than ever before.

Who chooses? The individual. The modern individual is not the peasant of yore with a fixed future yawning ahead. He (and now she, effectively doubling the market) is a battleground of decisions and preferences.

What follows from this is what I call the "California self." The self has been around for a long time, but what properties it has and how much it does varies with time and culture. I want to distinguish between a maximal self and a minimal self. The California self is the maximal self, a self who chooses, who feels pleasure and pain, who dictates action, who maximizes, and who even has things like esteem and efficacy. The California self has almost everything but a tan. Contrast the maximal self with the minimal self, the New England self. This is a self more like the self our grandparents had. It does little more than just behave; it is certainly not preoccupied with how it feels—if it feels at all.

So I have argued that our wealth, when coupled with a market for individualism, has produced the California self: An exalted entity whose pleasures and pains, whose successes and failures occupy center stage in our society. Such rampant individualism might be positive, bringing with it sweet freedoms, or it might at worst be innocuous. But the rise of the California self coincides with two sets of historical events which have so weakened our commitment to larger goods and to the commons that they have left our youth with only their California selves. And the California self, without the buffering of commitment to the commons, is, as we shall see, set up for depression.

The assassinations. Two sets of events have weakened the commitment of Americans to the commons as a means for achieving desired goals. Those of you who grew up in the early 1960s probably sensed what I sensed on November 22, 1963, as we watched our vision of the future destroyed by terrorism. We lost hope that our society could cure human ills. And a generation altered its commitment, out of fear and out of despair, from careers of public service to careers in which we could, at least, make ourselves happy as individuals. This shift from the public to the private was reinforced by the Martin Luther King, Jr., the Malcolm X, and the Robert Kennedy assassinations.

The Vietnam War taught those a bit younger the same lesson. The futility of 10 years of war eroded their commitment to patriotism and America. Watergate reinforced this. So a commitment to the nation was no longer viable enough to provide hope for the future on a large scale. I suggest that an erosion of commitment to the nation causes a rise in individuals' turning inward to look for satisfaction within their own lives. Our children ask what the world owes them, whereas our parents asked what they owed the world. It is more than a coincidence that some of those who turned their lives inward during the 1960s are in the 1980s those who write social science.

Loss of God and family. There are other institutions that might have replaced the nation as a source of hope and identity, keeping young people from turning inward to themselves. Religion and the family are two such buffers. But, interestingly, the erosion of belief in the nation coincided with a breakdown of the family (one of two marriages ends in divorce) and took place against a backdrop of a culture with little belief in God. So, add together the waning belief in God, the breakdown of the belief in the benevolence and power of America, and finally, the breakdown in the family. Where can one now turn for identity, for satisfaction, and for hope? To a very small and frail unit, indeed: the self.

Belief in the self, individualism, is viable against a background of belief in some large institutions—religion, country, family. When we fail in some of our personal goals, as we all must, we can fall back on these larger institutions for hope. Recall the stone-age Kaluli. When they fail, their integration within their tribe prevents loss from becoming hopelessness. With a commitment to the commons, present helplessness and personal failures do not get transformed into despair for the long future. In contrast, for the individual who is standing alone without the buffer of the larger beliefs, helplessness and failure become hopelessness and despair all too easily.

Learned Helplessness and Depression

I have proposed that the change in explanation of human action from the environment to the self within psychology mirrors a larger change within the society. The profitable market for the customization of goods to meet idiosyncratic tastes, coupled with the enormous spending power of the average American, has motivated a glorification of the individual. At the same time, the assassination of our liberal leaders, the war in Vietnam, and the dissolution of the family have produced an erosion of commitment to the commons. What remains is the hollow California self, preoccupied with its own hedonics, without larger institutions to fall back on when the self is thwarted.

How is all of this relevant to the epidemic of depression now upon us? I have argued for a number of years that depression is a disorder of the self. I have argued, in particular, that depression can ensue when individuals find themselves helpless to achieve their goals or to escape their frustrations (Seligman, 1975). When individuals face failures that they cannot control, they become helpless. When does helplessness expand to become full-blown depression? In this theory, when the person attributes failures to stable, global, and internal causes, helplessness becomes hopelessness and depression results (Abramson, Alloy, & Metalsky, 1988; Abramson, Seligman, & Teasdale, 1978; Peterson & Seligman, 1984).

Life is inevitably full of personal failures. Our stocks go down, people we love reject us, we write bad papers, we don't get the job we want, we give bad lectures. To begin with, an individualistic culture such as ours offers little in the way of Kaluli-type reciprocity between the society and the individual when loss occurs. Furthermore, the set of conditions I have just described maximizes the chances that these commonplace failures will be attributed to internal, stable, and global causes. The waxing of the individual produces internal attributions for failure, and the waning of the commons produces stable and global attributions for failure. To the extent that larger, benevolent institutions (God, nation, family) are no longer credited, personal failures are interpreted as catastrophic because they seem to last longer and to contaminate more of life. To the extent that such institutions command belief, any personal failure seems less eternal and less pervasively undermining. Either the waxing of individualism alone or the waning of the commons alone would increase the vulnerability to depression. That the two have coincided in America's recent history is, in my analysis, the source of the epidemic of depression.

The Future of Individualism

Both in psychology and, more important, in American society, we now live in the age of the individual. What is the long-term future of individualism? What is the long-term future of the psychology of personal control, which has become quite fashionable in the last two decades?

I suggest that both the future of individualism and, consequently, the future of the psychology of personal control are quite limited (Seligman, in press). I think that rampant individualism carries with it two seeds of its own destruction. First, a society that exalts the individual to the extent that ours now does will be ridden with depression. Look at this situation in reinforcement terms: The doctrine of individualism is followed by the punishment of a tenfold increase in depression. People will thus become less likely to hold this doctrine.

Second, and perhaps more important, is meaninglessness. I am not going to be foolish enough to attempt to define *meaning* for you. But surely one necessary condition for meaning (assuredly not sufficient) is the attachment to something larger than oneself (Nozick, 1981). And the larger the entity, the more meaning there is to be derived. To the extent that it is now difficult for young people to take seriously their relationship with God, to care about their relationship with the country, or to be part of a large and abiding family, meaning in life will be very difficult to find. The self, to put it another way, is a very poor site for meaning.

So individualism without commitment to the commons produces depression and meaninglessness on a massive scale. If this is so, something has to change. What?

One possibility is that individualism will wane, that the California self will transmogrify back into the New England self. Another, more frightening possibility is that we will rashly surrender the sweet freedoms that individualism brings and will give up personal control and concern for the self in order to shed depression and attain meaning. The twentieth century is riddled with disastrous examples of societies that have done just this to cure their ills. The current yearning for fundamentalist religion both in America and throughout the world appears to represent such a tempation.

There is a final possibility, a more hopeful one: One property of the California self is that it is self-improving. It has become convinced that jogging, while inconvenient, is in the long run good for its well-being. Perhaps it can now be convinced that its inordinate preoccupaton with itself is bad for its well-being in the long run. It might then choose to scale down its own importance. Perhaps we could retain our belief in the importance of the individual while diminishing our preoccupation with our own comfort and discomfort and, at the same time, balancing this with a renewed commitment to the commons. A balance between individualism, with its perilous freedoms, and commitment to the common good should both lower depression and make life more meaningful.

In this age of choice, this choice, surely, is ours.

References

Abramson, L. Y., Alloy, L. B., & Metalsky, G. I. (1989). The cognitive diathesis-stress theories of depression: Toward an adequate evaluation of the theories' validities. In L. B. Alloy (Ed.), *Cognitive processes in depression* (pp. 3-30). New York: Guilford Press.

Abramson, L. Y., Seligman, M.E.P., & Teasdale, J. (1978). Learned helplessness in humans: Critique and reformulation. *Journal of Abnormal Psychology, 87,* 49-59.

Egeland, J. A., & Hostetter, A. M. (1983). Amish Study I: Affective disorders among the Amish, 1976-1980. *American Journal of Psychiatry, 140,* 56-61.

Egeland, J. A., Hostetter, A. M., & Eshleman, S. K. (1983). Amish Study III: The impact of cultural factors on diagnosis of bipolar illness. *American Journal of Psychiatry, 140,* 67-71.

Kleinman, A. (1982). Neurasthenia and depression: A study of somatization and culture in China. *Cultural and Medical Psychiatry, 6,* 117-190.

Klerman, G. (1979, April). The age of melancholy. *Psychology Today,* 37-88.

Klerman, G. (1988). The current age of youthful melancholia. *British Journal of Psychiatry, 152,* 4-14.

Klerman, G., Lavori, P., Rice, J., Reich, T., Endicott, J., Andreasen, N., Keller, M., & Hirschfeld, R. (1985). Birth cohort trends in rates of major depressive disorder among relatives of patients with affective disorder. *Archives of General Psychiatry, 42,* 689-693.

Murphy, J., Sobol, A., Neff, R., Olivier, D., & Leighton, A. (1984). Stability of prevalence: Depression and anxiety disorders. *Archives of General Psychiatry, 41,* 990-997.

Myers, J., Weissman, M., Tischler, G., Holzer, C., Leaf, P., Orvaschel, H., Anthony, J., Boyd, J., Burke, J., Kramer, M., & Stoltzman, R. (1984). Six-month prevalence of psychiatric disorders in three communities. *Archives of General Psychiatry, 41,* 959-967.

Nozick, R. (1981). *Philosophical explanations.* Cambridge, MA: Belknap Press.

Peterson, C., & Seligman, M.E.P. (1984). Causal explanations as a risk factor for depression: Theory and evidence. *Psychological Review, 91,* 347-374.

Peterson, C., Seligman, M.E.P., & Vaillant, G. (1988). Pessimistic explanatory style as a risk factor for physical illness: A thirty-five year longitudinal study. *Journal of Personality and Social Psychology, 55,* 23-27.

Reich, T., Van Eerdewegh, P., Rice, J., Mullaney, J., Klerman, G., & Endicott, J. (1987). The family transmission of primary major depressive disorder. *Journal of Psychiatric Research, 21*(4), 613-624.

Robins, L., Helzer, J., Weissman, M., Orvaschel, H., Gruenberg, E., Burke, J., & Regier, D. (1984). Lifetime prevalence of specific psychiatric disorders in three sites. *Archives of General Psychiatry, 41,* 949-958.
Scheiffelin, E. (1984). *The cultural analysis of depressive affect: An example from New Guinea.* Unpublished manuscript, University of Pennsylvania.
Seligman, M.E.P. (1975). *Helplessness: On depression, development, and death.* San Francisco: Freeman.
Seligman, M.E.P. (in press). *Learned optimism.* New York: Knopf.

MICHAEL J. MAHONEY

SPORT PSYCHOLOGY

Michael J. Mahoney received his PhD from Stanford University and is now a professor of counseling psychology at the University of California at Santa Barbara. The author of 12 books and numerous scientific articles, Mahoney helped pioneer the "cognitive revolution" in psychology, and he continues to contribute to the growing interface between the cognitive and clinical sciences.

Honored as a Fellow by the American Psychological Association, he was chosen to be a Master Lecturer on the Psychotherapy Process in 1981. His professional awards include a Fulbright Award in 1984, the Faculty Scholar Medal from Pennsylvania State University in 1982, and a 1985 Citation Classic from Science Citation Index in recognition of the influence of his 1974 book *Cognition and Behavior Modification*.

Mahoney has served on the editorial boards of 12 scientific journals. In addition, he has worked with the U.S. Olympic Committee in the area of sport psychology since 1978. His research interests include basic processes in psychological development and psychotherapy, theoretical and philosophical issues, psychology of science, and health and sport psychology. His forthcoming book, *Human Change Processes: Notes on the Facilitation of Personal Development,* attempts to integrate the research literature from several disciplines as they bear on the conceptualization and facilitation of psychological change. An active athlete, Mahoney was a 1988 National Master's Champion in U.S. Olympic Weightlifting.

MICHAEL J. MAHONEY

SPORT PSYCHOLOGY

Recreational activities and organized sports have been a part of human civilization since its earliest recorded emergence. In fact, as comparative psychologists have noted, activities that appear to be playful occur in most mammalian species, with their prevalence increasing as one moves toward the primates and hominids (McFarland, 1987). In the case of humans, the evidence is now quite extensive: Recreational play and athletics are integral to healthy personality development, and they are very important elements of societal and cultural development as well.

In what follows, I shall outline the major contours of the specialization called *sport psychology* as I currently understand it. After a brief overview of its history, I shall focus on psychological studies of exceptional athletes and the skills involved in peak athletic performance. Psychological services in sport will then be sketched, followed by a discussion of human rights in recreation. I will conclude with a brief but emphatic affirmation of sport psychology as a newly recognized specialization that has already made important contributions to our understanding of human nature in action.

I am indebted to the U.S. Olympic Committee and the U.S. Weightlifting Federation for their research support.

Historical Context

Any introductory discussion of sport psychology should address a paradox that characterizes this field: Its conceptual roots lie in prehistoric antiquity, yet it has only recently become a visible and popular area of inquiry. The Olympic Games were revived in 1896, but the ancient Olympics survived more than a thousand years, from 776 B.C. to 393 A.D. (Segrave & Chu, 1981). Likewise, various forms of what are now called the martial arts had been developed and refined in the Far East during the first two millennia before Christ. In both Greek and Asian cultures, the interdependence of mind and body was not only acknowledged, but emphasized as central to both performance and personal development. If athletes and coaches of these ancient cultures recognized this link, why has it taken so long to become a formally recognized area of scientific inquiry?

There are a number of possible responses to that question, and it is likely that more than one factor has been involved in the belatedness of our formalizing the field now called sport psychology. Science itself, we should recall, did not become a powerful influence until the last three centuries. Moreover, athletic competitions did not become a medium of international exchange in modern times until late in the 19th century. For better or worse, discovering psychological aids to winning has been motivated in part by political, economic, and ideological rivalries. Indeed, athletic competitions (particularly the Olympic Games and world championships) have been badly abused by governments seeking to demonstrate the superiority of their race or political ideology. This was illustrated quite dramatically by Adolf Hitler at the 1936 Berlin Olympics, and it was one of the reasons that Jesse Owens' four gold medals there meant so much to those who opposed racism and fascism. I shall return later to the problems that stem from exaggerating the importance of winning and the abuse of sports in our culture.

Without belaboring speculation as to why sport psychology is such a recently formalized discipline, let me suggest that a major obstacle to its development across the centuries has been the continuing dualism in Western thought—the separation of mind and body—which has only recently begun to be challenged within psychology. Although René Descartes (1596–1650) is often blamed for the formalization of that dualism, it was actually Plato (427–347 B.C.) who first explicitly proposed that we separate the domains of reflective thought and reflexive flesh. Plato spoke of the "rabble of the senses" and warned against assigning too much importance to the sensations and experiences of the body (Mahoney, in press; W. J. Morgan & Meier, 1988; Weiss, 1969). From a philosophical standpoint, that attitude remained dominant until the emergence of empirical science in the

17th century, and its impact on our understanding has yet to be fully appreciated, let alone reduced.

The Scientific Origins of Sport Psychology

The impetus toward reconnecting body and brain through sport emerged primarily during the present century. Although the origins of modern sport psychology lie primarily within the domains of physical education and exercise science, many of the earliest and most influential investigations in the field were conducted by psychologists who had developed a special interest in sports and recreation. The first reported experiment in the field, for example, was by Indiana University psychologist Norman Triplett (1897). Triplett noticed that cyclists seemed to perform better when they raced against someone else (rather than alone, against time). He designed an ingenious laboratory experiment to test various hypotheses and found that his experimental subjects did, indeed, show marked improvements in racing time when they competed against another contestant.

The founder of sport psychology in the United States was Coleman Roberts Griffith, who, with the support of George Huff, established the first laboratory for sport psychology research at the University of Illinois in 1925. Besides studying athletes' reaction times and flexibility, Griffith corresponded with Notre Dame football coach Knute Rockne about psychological and motivational aspects of coaching and athletics. He later served as team psychologist and researcher for the Chicago Cubs baseball team. Griffith also interviewed Harold E. ("Red") Grange after Grange scored four touchdowns in the first 12 minutes of the 1924 Illinois–Michigan football game. The incident is worth noting because it illustrates how advanced Griffith was in examining psychological processes in sports performance (Kroll & Lewis, 1970).

Grange had turned in an incredible performance during that game, scoring four touchdowns the first four times he handled the ball. Two of his runs were kickoff returns of 95 and 67 yards. Perhaps out of kindness to the Michigan team, the Illinois coach took Grange out of the game after his fourth run. When he returned in the fourth quarter, he ran for a fifth touchdown and passed 18 yards for a sixth. The psychological twist to all of this came when Griffith interviewed him after the game: Grange had no recall of any of his spectacular runs. As modern athletes often report, Grange was at a loss to describe his experience during the game. This led Griffith to write later about the "automatic skill response." In today's language, he was pioneering the study of what has come to be called variously the "hot streak," "groove," "flow," or the "sweet spot in time" (Csikszentmihalyi, 1975; M. Csikszentmihalyi & I. S. Csikszentmihalyi,

1988; Jerome, 1980; Leonard, 1974; Maslow, 1968; Murphy & White, 1978). These "automatic" and "unconscious" executions of highly developed skills remain a topic of current research and theory on peak performance.

Although there was some activity in sport psychology between the 1920s and 1960s, it was sparse relative to what has occurred since then. Interviews with sport scientists from Europe and the Soviet Union also suggest that centers for research and teaching in the area of sport psychology were beginning to spread beyond Rome, Berlin, and Leningrad during the second quarter of this century, but details of these developments are not yet available in English.[1]

Modern Sport Psychology

The dawning of the modern era in sport psychology was reflected in two important developments: The First International Congress of Sport Psychology was held in Rome in 1965, and in 1967 the North American Society for Psychology of Sport and Physical Activity was founded. Interest and activity in the area continued to accelerate throughout the 1970s, becoming especially apparent soon after the 1976 Olympics in Montreal. In a media interview during those Games, world record holder Mark Spitz commented that—at the Olympic level of competition—physical skill differences are minimal relative to the importance of mental factors. An increasing number of athletes and coaches seemed to agree, as reflected by their growing interest in developing a psychological edge over their competitors. Fueling that interest was a rumor that the Soviets had employed more than 90 sport psychologists to help prepare their teams for the Montreal Olympics.

In 1978 the U.S. Olympic Committee recruited expert advisers in four branches of sport science: biomechanics, exercise physiology, nutrition, and sport psychology. Later they established an official Sport Psychology Committee and a Registry, in which, after intensive review of individuals' training and experience, they recognized three nonexclusive categories of sport psychologists: research, educational, and clinical. Sport psychology played a more visible role in the 1984 Los Angeles Olympics, with the American Broadcasting Company (ABC) showing a series of excerpts on the topic throughout its television coverage. Several of the U.S. teams had established ongoing consultations with sport psychologists, many of whom were in attendance at the Games. A walk-in clinic was set up by several sport psychologists near the athletes' living quarters; it was kept very busy. In 1984 sport psychologists were not recognized as essential medical staff, however, and they were denied access to backstage areas at the competition, as well as to the Olympic Village, where athletes were staying. This distressed a number of athletes and coaches (not to mention sport psychologists), and—much to their credit—the U.S. Olympic Committee sent two official, fully credentialed sport psychologists to the 1988 Games in Seoul.

The number of individuals specializing (and respecializing) in sport psychology has increased dramatically over the last few years, and this trend has yet to plateau. As will be illustrated, the range of topics, research questions, and services in this area also continues to grow. It is, to be sure, an exciting time of expansion and exploration, and it touches upon some of the most fundamental mysteries of mental and physical integration. Broadly defined, sport psychology is the scientific study and application of psychological principles in the realms of recreation and athletics.

Psychological Studies of Exceptional Athletes

Our enjoyment of and fascination with sports is deep, universal, enduring, and complex. One clearly identifiable theme in both lay and professional interest, however, has been our fascination with the personalities and characteristics of great athletes. Griffith's early correspondence with Rockne and interview with Grange are of interest, in part, because they help illuminate those personalities to us. Beginning with Vanek and Cratty's (1970) classic volume on psychology and the superior athlete, sport researchers have tried to refine our understanding of the psychological profile of elite (world-class) athletes. The methodologies and assumptions of these researchers have varied, of course, and these variations merit at least brief comment.

Sport Personology and the Trait–Skill Controversy

A controversy that emerged within the field of sport psychology during the 1970s had to do with the quest to identify a general athletic personality. The instruments used in that quest were also debated, because the most popular had been developed primarily for use in assessing patterns and degrees of psychopathology as well as personality makeup—the Minnesota Multiphasic Personality Inventory (MMPI), the California Psychological Inventory (CPI), the Maudsley Personality Inventory (MPI), and the Cattell 16PF IPAT. The debate began to polarize with the modern resurgence of experimental sport psychology. Those who came to be called *sport personologists* defended a personality-trait approach, while others in the field challenged their contentions and proposed alternative measures and models that emphasized psychological skills (that were modifiable) rather than unchanging traits (Fisher, 1976, 1984; Kane, 1978; Mahoney, 1979; Morgan, 1978, 1980; Martens, 1975; Ogilvie, 1968; Ryan, 1976; and Silva, 1984). The controversy seems to have subsided substantially in the last few years, however, with an increasing number of sport psychologists adopting an "interactionist" perspective and acknowledging that measures of enduring personality traits and modifiable skills may be usefully employed in combination. I shall focus here on representative studies of the personality traits of the exceptional athlete; studies focused more directly on psychological skills will be addressed in the next section.

Psychological profiles of the elite athlete have reflected the abovementioned differences in methodologies and models (Gould, Weiss, & Weinberg, 1981; Highlen & Bennett, 1979; Morgan, 1985; Morgan & Pollock, 1977; Ogilvie, 1968). After reviewing a number of studies that employed traditional measures of personality and psychopathology, for example, Ogilvie (1968) offered the following portrayal:

> The studies reviewed strongly support the tendency for certain personality traits to receive greater reinforcement within the competitive world of athletics . . . .We can state with some certitude that those who retain their motivation for competition will have most of the following personality traits: ambition, organization, deference, dominance, endurance, and aggression. There will be fewer introverted types in adult-level competition. Emotional maturity will span a range from average to high average and be complemented by self-control, self-confidence, tough-mindedness, trustfulness, intelligence, high conscience development, and low levels of tension. (p. 161)

There are differences, however, in the profiles suggested by other researchers and reviewers. Hemery (1986), for example, painted a somewhat different portrait of the elite athlete, based on his series of intensive interviews with 63 world-class athletes from 22 sports and 12 countries. His interviewees included Sebastian Coe, Bob Cousy, Wayne Gretzky, John Havlicek, Billie Jean King, Rod Laver, Carl Lewis, Chris Evert Lloyd, Edwin Moses, Al Oerter, Arnold Palmer, Pete Rose, O. J. Simpson, and Jackie Stewart. After two years of interviewing and interpretation, Hemery concluded that:

> Most of the athletes had started out as shy, sometimes self-conscious, introverts. In several cases, sport provided an avenue through which they became far more outgoing; their sporting success strengthened their self-image and in many cases diminished their shyness. Obviously, because of their notoriety, the

> majority have a learned public exterior. Nevertheless, many still identify themselves as being quite shy, introverted people today. (1986, pp. 199–200)

In this sample, at least, dominance, aggressiveness, and extroversion were not typical patterns. Hemery found that those athletes who had gone on to succeed in other areas of life (e.g., as sports announcers) did view themselves as more socially outgoing.

Although Hemery's methods and conclusions are open to criticism, his is one of the few attempts to place outstanding athletic achievements in a developmental, life history perspective. Thus, he reported that his sample of athletes described their childhood and upbringing as happy, secure, stable, and nurturant; the majority of the athletes had maintained a close and positive relationship with their parents and their families. As I discuss in a later section, responsible parenting involves supporting but not forcing sports participation. The stresses associated with excessive parental pressure to succeed may actually be an obstacle to sports achievement, as well as detrimental to the well-being of the young athlete.

Consistent with other research on the psychological skills of world-class athletes discussed in the section that follows, Hemery also found that his interviewees were generally very confident and reported well-developed abilities to concentrate, especially under pressure. They also acknowledged that they were tense or nervous before important competitions, but that they expected and accepted this as part of their job, and some noted that their anxiety actually helped their performance. Finally, Hemery's sample of athletes unanimously reported total mental involvement in their sport, emphasizing the importance of mental training and mental preparations prior to competitions.

The "Iceberg Profile" of the Elite Athlete

A more quantitative profile of the elite athlete was offered by W. P. Morgan (1985a). After a series of studies spanning a decade and sampling over a dozen sports, Morgan formulated a mental health model of human performance:

> The model specifies that *success in sport is inversely correlated with psychopathology.* Another way of presenting the basic thesis underlying the model would be to state that positive mental health is directly correlated with success in sport. The model predicts that anxious, depressed, neurotic, or schizoid athletes, for example, will be less successful in sport than individuals scoring within the normal range. (1985a, p. 71)

Morgan presented data consistent with this model, and he offered the "iceberg profile" as a general psychological depiction of the elite athlete.

As shown in Figure 1, the elite athletes tested by Morgan and his colleagues showed a distinctive pattern in their responses to the Profile of Mood States (POMS) (McNair, Lorr, & Droppleman, 1971). Compared with the general population, elite athletes scored relatively low on tension, depression, anger, fatigue, and confusion, and—at the tip of the pictorial iceberg—they scored much higher on vigor. Morgan urged caution in the interpretation and use of these findings, however, emphasizing that the magnitude of statistical relationships involved does not warrant the use of the POMS in the selection of athletes. Subsequent research has indicated that the POMS may be useful in monitoring changes within individual athletes, however, and in revealing some of the psychological changes associated with overtraining and burnout (Morgan, Brown, Raglin, O'Connor, & Ellickson, 1987).

Psychological Skills in Exceptional Athletes

It should not, perhaps, be surprising that the study of exceptional performance has also tended to focus on the performance skills of exceptional athletes. As was discussed earlier, and without forgetting the wide range of individual differences observed, elite athletes seem to be less anxious, more highly motivated, and more confident and vigorous than the general population. The question remains, however, as to how such characteristics might translate into superior competitive performances. How is it that these individuals accomplish what they do, often with remarkable consistency and excellence? Are some skills more important than others? Can they be developed? Research on the psychological skills that may contribute to peak performance has recently begun to sketch some preliminary answers to questions such as these.

An example is a recent national survey of 713 male and female athletes representing 23 sports (Mahoney, Gabriel, & Perkins, 1987). The sample included 126 elite athletes and, as a rigorous comparison group, 446 collegiate athletes. Each was asked to complete a 51-item self-report questionnaire focused on psychological skills. When the results were analyzed, they suggested substantial differences between groups, as shown in Figure 2.

Relative to their less successful peers, elite athletes reported being more highly motivated to do well and more reliant on internally referenced and kinesthetic mental preparations. The latter refers to the finding that successful athletes have been reported to use "whole body" imagery and "internal" imagery in their mental prep-

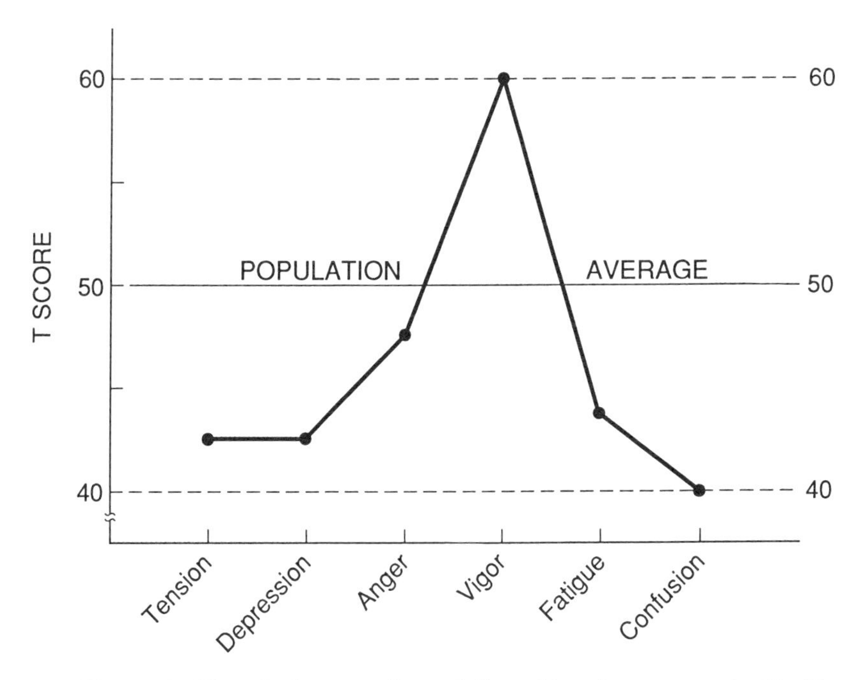

Figure 1. The iceberg profile of elite athletes' scores on the Profile of Mood States. Adapted from Morgan (1985a) with permission.

arations (see Mahoney & Avener, 1977). The elite group also reported fewer problems with performance anxiety, greater success in concentrating during competition, and higher levels of self-confidence. Although elite athletes also placed greater emphasis on team (vs. their own individual) performance, this last finding must be qualified depending on the type of sport involved.

Sports can be differentiated, for example, by the psychomotor challenge facing the athlete (Gentile, 1972). Closed sports are those in which that challenge remains relatively static (unchanging), usually because the task is to overcome a physical obstacle (such as time, distance, or gravity). Archery, bowling, golf, track and field, and weightlifting are examples of closed sports. By way of contrast, open sports are those in which the challenge facing the athlete is dynamic (changeable), usually because it involves one or more human opponents. Thus, all team sports are open (e.g., baseball, basketball, football), and a few individual sports are open (e.g., boxing, fencing, wrestling). As shown in Figure 3, the emphasis on team performance is significantly different in open versus closed sports. Overall, athletes in closed sports tended to report more problems with their confidence, concentration, and anxiety management than did their coun-

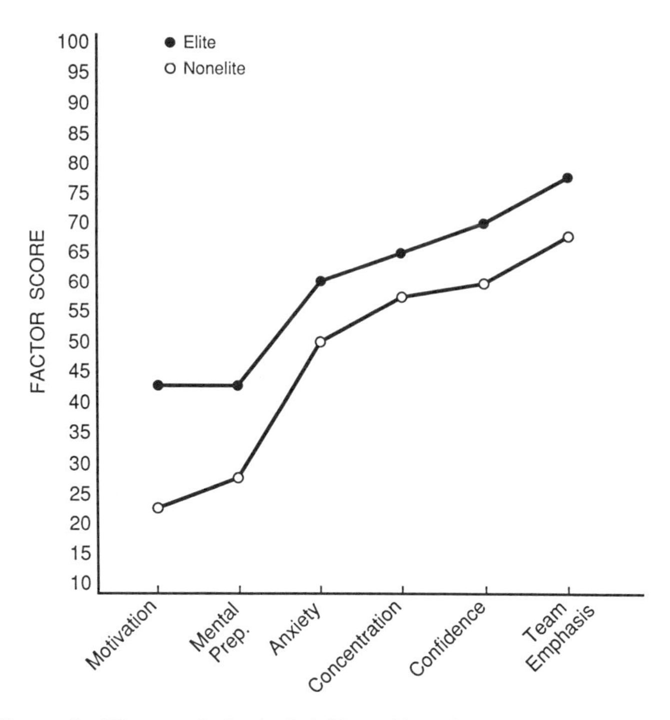

Figure 2. The psychological skill profiles of elite and nonelite athletes. From Mahoney, Gabriel, & Perkins (1987) with permission.

terparts in open sports. There is also some evidence that cognitive and motivational factors may influence individual preferences for particular sports (Sadalla, Linder, & Jenkins, 1988).

There were also some differences between the reports of the male and female athletes sampled in this study. Consistent with other research on gender differences in athletics, nonelite women athletes reported significantly lower levels of self-confidence and substantially greater problems with performance anxiety (see Figure 4).

Interestingly, however, these differences disappeared at the elite level. That is, those women who were among the best in their sport reported psychological skills and problems approximately equivalent to those reported by elite male athletes. This suggests the possibility that certain skills may be developed or refined en route to athletic excellence, or that increasingly difficult competition may select individuals, in part, on the basis of their psychological skill development. The existing research is still too preliminary to allow much more than informed conjecture on the nature and consequences of that development, but such conjecture is worth at least brief mention.

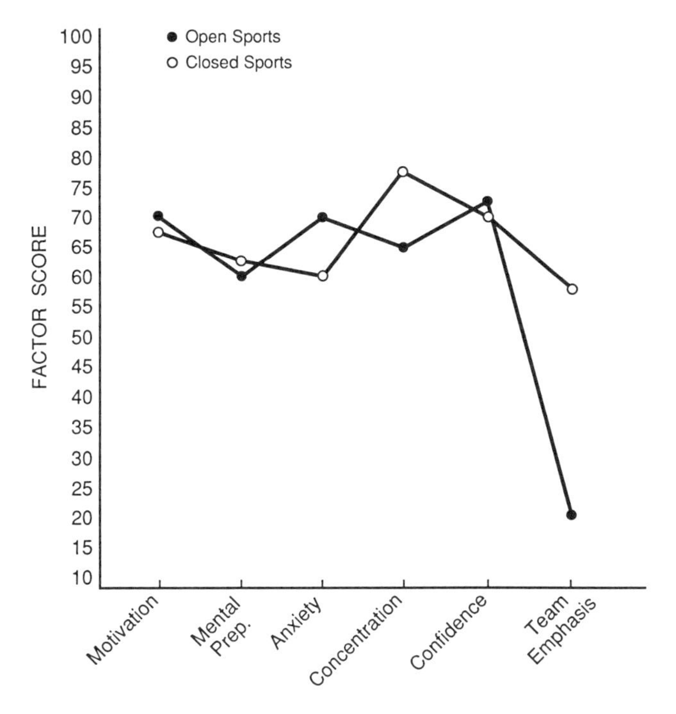

Figure 3. The psychological skill profiles of nonelite athletes in open and closed sports. From Mahoney, Gabriel, & Perkins (1987) with permission.

Psychological Studies of Peak Performance

Complementing their interest in the person and patterns of the exceptional athlete, an enduring fascination of sport psychologists, past and present, has been with the phenomenon of peak performance, those episodes of unusual ability that seem to punctuate all of our lives. What is it, in that complex coordination of psychobiological processes, that allows each of us to have our moments of unusually balanced and powerful movement? Why is it, for example, that after you have practiced a sport for a while, your average performance may gradually improve, but these improvements are punctuated and contrasted with slumps and streaks? On rare occasions, for example, you may find yourself performing well above your usual level—for example, bowling a game twice your average or knocking several strokes off your golf handicap. Or, in another context, how is it possible for humans to overcome and survive what appear to be insurmountable

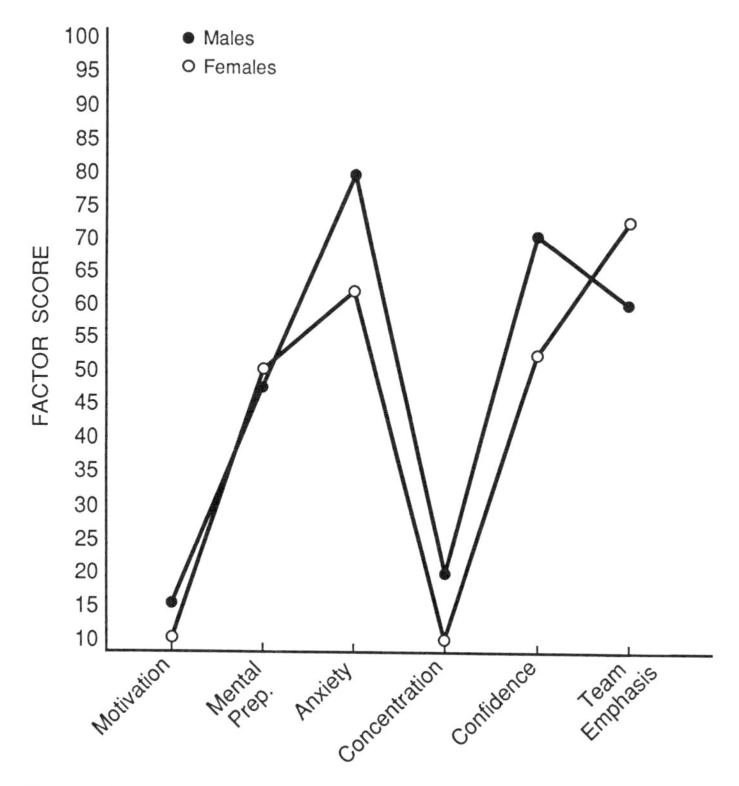

Figure 4. Psychological skill profiles of male and female nonelite athletes. From Mahoney, Gabriel, & Perkins (1987) with permission.

odds? How is it possible for a person weighing 50 kg (110 lb) to lift the end of an automobile 20 times heavier, and only when there was an urgent (life-contingent) need to do so (e.g., an injured child)? Whether rendered as expressions of the human body, brain, mind, or spirit, our interest in such phenomena is perennial.

Let me illustrate this point with a real-life example. At the 1982 U.S. Olympic Sports Festival in Indianapolis, Indiana, a young weightlifter named Derrick Crass was on his way to a winning performance. In his second of three possible attempts in the clean and jerk competition, he attempted the formidable feat of putting more than double his own bodyweight overhead. Weighing less than 90 kg (198 lb), Crass called for a weight of 187 kg (411 lb). He "cleaned" the weight to his chest in one quick and powerful movement, then drove it overhead and split underneath it (Figure 5a). That exhilarating moment was very brief, however, and then tragedy struck. The friction between the platform and his rear foot was insufficient for that weight; in an accident rare to the sport, over 400 pounds came crashing down on him, literally driving him into the platform (Figures 5b–5d).

Crass was unconscious when the barbell was lifted off him and an ambulance was called. There was grave concern about the extent of his internal injuries and for his life. He was loaded onto a stretcher and carried toward a door to await the ambulance. In a scene that may sound like it came from *Finnegan's Wake*, however, Crass not only

(a) (b) (c)

(d) (e) (f)

Figure 5. Weightlifter Derrick Crass (a) nearing completion of a double-bodyweight clean and jerk, (b-d) being driven to the platform by the weight, (e) successfully completing the lift less than three minutes later, and (f) balancing more than double his bodyweight on one leg. Photographs by Dave Black.

regained consciousness, but got off the stretcher and demanded his right to a third attempt at the weight! Those attending were dumbfounded. The trainer and attending physician could find no external signs of bone, muscle, or connective tissue injury. The timer was still running and indicated that less than a minute was left in the allotted three-minute interval.

Welcomed by an ovation just for being upright and in one piece, Crass rushed onto the platform and centered himself over the weight. A hush fell over the crowd when they realized that he meant business. And it was all over in a matter of seconds. He successfully cleaned the weight, took a short breath, jerked it overhead with a very assertive split, and then finished the lift by bringing his feet together in a parallel line (Figure 5e). And that was just the start! After he received the "down" signal from the center referee, Crass broke into a big smile and—to the click of cameras and the cheers of the crowd—leaning ever so slightly to one side, he lifted his other foot off the platform, and balanced more than twice his bodyweight on one leg (Figure 5f)!

There is, of course, a range of possible reactions to and interpretations of that incident of peak performance. On the personal side, Derrick Crass recovered from his bruised muscles and ribs and went on to represent the United States in the 1984 and 1988 Olympics. On the more scientific and theoretical side, we may ask any number of questions about the principles and processes that explain and make possible such a superhuman performance. Such questions have been asked by sport psychology researchers, and the findings to date offer some intriguing insights into the everyday and unusual capacities of humans at play.

Performance Anxiety

The anxiety and stress associated with competition and public performance have been a perennial concern of athletes and a common focus of sport psychologists. Until recently, the guiding assumption about the relationship between anxiety and performance was that rendered by the famous Yerkes-Dodson inverted U hypothesis (Yerkes & Dodson, 1908). That hypothesis states that very low and very high levels of anxiety are associated with poorer performances, while moderate levels of anxiety are more often linked to better performances. Without belaboring the extensive research literature addressed to this hypothesis, it now appears that it is a gross oversimplification (Mahoney & Meyers, 1989; Passer, 1984; Sonstroem, 1984). The original formulation actually focused on autonomic arousal rather than anxiety per se, and it is now clear that the two concepts are not the same (see Burton, 1988; Neiss, 1988). Moreover, as Oxendine (1970) and others have noted, the optimal levels of preperformance anxiety may well depend on the psychomotor demands of different sports (e.g., golf versus weightlifting), not to mention individual differences and preferences. The latter appear to be considerable, and there is increasing evidence that absolute level of anxiety may be less important than the personal meaning of that anxiety, as well as what the athlete does in relation to it. The self-reports of elite athletes, for example, suggest that, relative to their less successful competitors, they: "(a) tend to view their anxiety as, at worst, a nuisance and, at best, an ally in their performance; (b) tend to 'pace' their pre-competition anxiety more effectively; and (c) are less focused on their anxiety and more focused on momentary task demands during their performance" (Mahoney & Meyers, 1989, p. 87).

In other words, peak performers report being less likely to experience their anxiety as an enemy, and they seem to be less vulnerable to the phenomenon of anxiety-induced anxiety (i.e., panicking over how anxious they feel). In fact, many report that they become concerned if their anxiety level is not high enough. Moreover, these athletes have sometimes related that they try to channel their high energy into their performance and that their anxiety tends to peak in the final stages of preparation and to stabilize or decline once they have engaged in their task (see Fenz, 1988). They also report that they are less distracted and distressed by mistakes during competition and that they strive to maintain full concentration on immediate task demands.

Concentration Skills

Peak performers also seem to have developed exceptional concentration abilities appropriate to their sport. They sometimes report being unaware of the audience and fully absorbed by the demands of their performance. Moreover, they relate that at times their movements become fluid and automatic, and their performance just seems to flow. This phenomenon of *flow* is worth elaborating on a bit.

In the tradition of Griffith's interview with Red Grange and his study of the automatic skill response, modern sport psychologists have remained fascinated with the psychological aspects of episodes of peak performance. As noted earlier, one does not need to be a world champion or sports superstar to experience those episodes; they seem to occur at least occasionally in the execution of a wide range of familiar movements in our everyday lives (M. Csikszentmihalyi & I. S. Csikszentmihalyi, 1988). The characteristics of the flow experience include the following:

1. It is experienced as an altered state of consciousness in which an unusual body-brain integration is achieved.

2. There is often a sense of timelessness.

3. Even during strenuous exercise, there is a sense of effortlessness sometimes described as like being on automatic pilot.

4. Becoming aware of and/or trying to control the flow (e.g., to extend it) often results in its disappearance.

5. Flow is something that can be allowed to happen, but even the most successful athletes report an inability to produce it at will.

Recent research has begun to suggest that attentional processes or concentration skills may play a central role in such phenomena. One example is the research reported by Landers and his colleagues on physiological and attentional processes in elite riflery experts (Hatfield, Landers, & Ray, 1987; Landers, Christina, Hatfield, Daniels, & Doyle, 1980). They found that many of the world-class athletes in this sport had spontaneously developed an ability to detect their own heartbeat and that, when their performance was at its best, they were systematically pulling the trigger just before ventricular contractions. Because the trajectory of the bullet is affected by even minor movements, this pattern of shooting between heartbeats produced the most consistent and positive results. Although the researchers did not inquire about experiencing flow, their data lend valuable information as to how well-developed attentional capacities may contribute to peak performances.

Another example comes from the study of world-class distance runners and their strategic use of concentration skills (W. P. Morgan & Pollack, 1977). In prior research Morgan had found that marathon runners often cognitively dissociate from sensory input during training and competition. In other words, in order to endure the pain (and especially get past "the wall") associated with such prolonged exertion, marathon runners frequently engage in cognitive activities that help distract them from what they are feeling. One runner reported that he did a life review during each race, beginning with his memories of first grade and then gradually proceeding year by year. Another wrote imaginary letters to family and friends, and a third listened to a full stack of Beethoven records. Individual strategies varied in content, but they all served the function of dissociation.

Interestingly, however, the elite group of runners did not engage in such dissociative strategies during their races. Although some reported having used such distractions earlier in their running careers, the world-class marathoners in this study said that they had abandoned that practice and now paid close attention to the feedback from their bodies—which, by the way, they did not experience as painful, but as necessary and strategic to their running efficiency. Subsequent laboratory experiments have begun to refine our understanding of these differences in concentration strategies (e.g., W. P. Morgan, 1985b).

Confidence

There is fairly consistent evidence that more successful athletes also tend to be more confident than less successful athletes (e.g., Highlen & Bennett, 1979), but the nature of the relationship between confidence and performance remains a focus of modern research. As documented by Feltz (1988), the experience of confidence is highly individualized and often specific to the challenge being confronted. Extending Bandura's (1977, 1982, 1986) theory of self-efficacy, Feltz and her colleagues have conducted some of the most sophisticated efforts to clarify the relationship between a person's momentary sense of ability and his or her actual performance. A range of clinical and anecdotal commentaries on the experience of confidence is consistent with her analysis.

At present, it would appear that confidence is a highly personalized experience, with both general and specific correlates. A successful or winning competition does not always increase subjective confidence, and this may depend on the psychological makeup of the athlete and the quality of the success experience (e.g., easy vs. difficult victory, important vs. unimportant contest, and so forth) (Vealey, 1986). Interviews with world champions (e.g., Hemery, 1986) across a wide range of sports suggest that—whatever else it may be—*confidence is not the simple absence of self-doubt.* On the contrary, their reports suggest that confidence, akin to the concept of courage, is a willingness to risk performance. In other words, world champions rarely report their experience of confidence as one of total and unwavering certainty of success or the absence of self-doubts. Like their less successful counterparts, they, too, report experiencing "mind chatter" and hesitations as they approach their challenge.

Self-confident athletes generally report the following:

1. A willingness, and even eagerness, to risk competition.
2. An awareness of self-doubts combined with an ability to remain primarily focused on the immediate demands of performance.
3. A more developed perspective on the importance of the outcome of any given competition, with some individuals emphasizing their value as a person as being independent of their success in any given performance.

The abovementioned perspective tends to be more common when athletes remain focused on the optimal *form* of their performance—in other words, the process of performing—rather than on the outcome or consequences of that performance. This is, after all, the literal meaning of *performance*: from the Latin *per formare*; literally, "to give form." Moreover, as I like to emphasize in consultations with athletes and coaches, the basic meaning of the term *self-confidence* can also be illuminated by looking at its roots. The term *confidence* comes from the Latin *con fidere,* meaning "with fidelity." Hence, it appears that people who remain faithful to themselves—positive and affirming in their self-regard irrespective of any specific successes and failures—may ironically be more likely to render more exceptional performances.

Motivation

Motivation is another of those familiar psychological concepts that becomes increasingly complex as its scientific investigation is refined. A variety of definitions have been offered that emphasize the maintenance or intensification of effortful activity, and theories of motivation as they apply to sports have usually been elaborations of more general models of human emotionality, intentionality, and learning (Roberts, 1984; Weinberg, 1984a). Among the issues under study in this area are the relative contribution of external versus internal (intrinsic) rewards for sports participation, the motivational elements of team membership and public performance, and the relative importance of short- and long-term goal setting in athletic training and skill development (Dishman, Ickes, & Morgan, 1980; Hall & Byrne, 1988; Locke & Latham, 1985).

Athletes' self-reports generally reflect that reasonable and personally meaningful goals are often experienced as helpful in training, but individual differences and developmental complexities must again be acknowledged. The motivation to participate in sports may change with other life developments, and the meaning of success may change in the very process of becoming successful. Contrary to some media portrayals, for example, athletes who drive themselves single-mindedly toward improvement may actually fare less well than those who seek that improvement in a more balanced context of overall life priorities. Athletes and coaches have become increasingly aware that a frequent source of motivational slumps and staleness may be overtraining and athletes' pushing themselves too hard (W. P. Morgan, Brown, Raglin, O'Connor, & Ellickson, 1987; R. E. Smith, 1986).

Mental Preparation

The final group of psychological skills relevant to exceptional performance to be discussed here involves the mental preparations performed by athletes in anticipation of actual competition. Two overlapping but separate subsets of theory and research can be invoked here: those having to do with last-minute preparations and those focusing on mental rehearsal, mental practice, and imagery.

With regard to the former, some preliminary generalizations seem warranted. Put simply, athletes perform more poorly when they are prevented from executing their usual last-minute "psyching" or "centering" strategies (Shelton & Mahoney, 1978; Weinberg, 1984b). On the other hand, there are wide individual differences in the content and apparent effectiveness of those strategies. Depending on the sport and the individual, last-minute preparatory rituals may be intended to amplify or dampen physiological arousal, to bolster confidence, or to focus concentration. Experienced athletes sometimes report that these final preparations help them increase their body–brain integration and their total absorption in their performance (Jerome, 1980). The mechanisms by which this might be accomplished remain to be clarified.

The research literature on mental rehearsal or mental practice is both extensive and somewhat confusing (Corbin, 1972; Feltz & Landers, 1983; Richardson, 1967a, 1967b; Suinn, 1985). Over 100 studies of mental practice have been reported, but they range widely in methodological quality and findings. On average, it appears that rehearsing a performance mentally can be beneficial, particularly when the individual is already physically familiar with the task and at a moderate level of skill development. Combining mental practice with physical practice may have some advantages over either in isolation. These generalizations must again be qualified, however, given the range of individual differences observed.

Interviews with successful athletes suggest that many individuals spontaneously develop their own styles of rehearsing and preparing for competitive performances. Noteworthy in their self-reports is the fact that mental imagery is not confined to visualizing a performance. Although additional research is needed, it now appears that many exceptional athletes employ a whole-body form of mental practice, rehearsing not only what they might see during a performance but also the feeling of their movements, as well as the sounds and smells of the competition. One focus of recent studies in this area has been the relation between self-reported mental rehearsal and patterns of brain and muscular activity (Epstein, 1980; Hale, 1982; Harris & Robinson, 1986; Hatfield & Landers, 1987).

Psychological Services in Sport

The psychological services that have been offered to athletes and coaches over the years can be grouped into three broad categories: (a) academic counseling, (b) skills training for performance enhancement, and (c) clinical services focused on adjustment and personal development.

Academic Counseling

Although academic counseling is seldom considered a part of sport psychology per se, it is probably the most common form of counseling offered to collegiate athletes, and it touches on a combination of psychological, social, and ethical issues. As a number of writers have noted, some institutions have offered academic counseling primarily to keep their athletes eligible for NCAA competition rather than because of a genuine interest in those athletes' education (Underwood, 1984; Waicukauski, 1982). Academic counseling services are now a regular component of most major college and university athletic programs. An important concern has been the fact that a sizable proportion of minority students on athletic scholarships have failed to complete their college degree programs. Advocates of reform have pointed out that many such athletes are simply exploited by college athletic programs, only to be ignored or abandoned once their eligibility is past or they otherwise become less valuable to their team.

Although only a small portion of the academic counselors who assist athletes are also specialists in sport psychology, the magnitude and ethical complexity of the issues involved here deserve the attention and involvement of all sport science and education professionals. As noted below, the student athlete's needs and rights are not neatly separable into academic, athletic, and psychological categories.

Skills Training for Performance Enhancement

Performance enhancement is a second broad category of psychological services that has recently become more popular and available to athletes of all ages and skill levels. There is now a variety of self-help books and audiovisual aids aimed at helping coaches and athletes identify and refine their development of skills in anxiety management, self-confidence, concentration, mental rehearsal, and motivation (e.g., Gauron, 1984; D. V. Harris & B. L. Harris, 1984; Lee & Owen, 1986; Mahoney, 1988; Martens, 1987; Nideffer, 1976; Orlick, 1980; Syer & Connolly, 1984; Tutko & Tosi, 1976; Unesthal, 1980; Waitley, 1980). Likewise, a growing number of institutions and agencies have begun to offer educational workshops and peak-performance seminars for the interested public.

Although there are benefits that may accrue from this increased visibility and availability of skills training programs, some sport psychologists have voiced concerns about aspects of these trade books and commercial programs. One concern has to do with the wisdom and ethics of offering practical and prescriptive guidelines that often go well beyond the current base of scientific evidence. This is, of course, a perennial problem in the realm of self-help programs and bibliotherapy (Rosen, 1987). Another concern has to do with the boundary between educational and clinical services, and the separability of an athlete's performance from his or her personal psychological functioning.

Personal Counseling and Clinical Services

Even though athletes in general and exceptional athletes in particular tend to score as psychologically healthier than their peers, there is no question that these same individuals may occasionally desire or require the services of a mental health professional. As Heyman (1986) and May (1986) have noted, athletes are hardly immune to the stresses and struggles of life span development, and some of their problems are most appropriately served only by licensed psychologists and psychiatrists. This issue stimulated some controversy several years ago when sport psychologists debated the issues of licensing and certification in the field (Danish & Hale, 1981; Harrison & Feltz, 1979; Heyman, 1984).[2]

The life problems and adjustment patterns that most frequently bring an athlete to the attention of a mental health professional are not all that different from those that affect the nonathlete. These include anxiety disorders, depression, substance abuse, eating disorders, relationship and identity issues, and burnout. There are also some patterns that have parallels in everyday life but that may be accentuated in the high-pressure and generally brief sporting careers of both amateur and professional athletes. Retirement can occur as early as the late teens in some sports, for example, and there is some reason to believe that athletes may be particularly vulnerable to developing substance abuse problems (because of the temptation of performance-enhancing drugs or, alternately, because of the illusion of physical invulnerablility, which may reduce the athlete's awareness of a developing drug problem). Psychological treatment of athletes must also be modified to meet the demands of their individual circumstances (e.g., some forms of chemotherapy involve banned substances, some athletes are on the road for weeks at a time, and so on).

There should be no doubt that competitive athletics can be stressful and that professional athletics often reflects an amplification of the potential risks and rewards involved at the amateur level. Some individuals do suffer from their experiences in the context of sports competition, especially the young and immature, when they are forced to take risks beyond their desire and ability. But this fact should not blind us to the aesthetic and existential challenges embodied in all recreation and sports. Because of my own fascination with the phenomena of peak performance and the frontiers of integrated (body-brain) activity, I have thus far selectively highlighted the exceptional over the ordinary and the elite over the average in this presentation. I shall try to redress that imbalance in the next section.

Human Rights and Recreation

I shall now establish the context for some of the issues that are at the forefront of research and theory about human play in all forms and at all levels. Three formative research areas will be briefly mentioned: youth sports, gender and meaning in sports, and exercise and health.

Youth Sports

Although developmental psychologists continue to speculate about the functions of play, there is little debate over the universality of games and their importance in human development (Bretherton, 1984; Fein, 1981; Leslie, 1987; Piaget, 1962). In analyses of the emergence of different forms of play across the life span, some differentiations have been offered. Coakley (1980), for example, suggested that distinctions be made among play, games, and sport. In his model, *play* is more spontaneous and individually expressive and *games*, although competitive, tend to emphasize interpersonal skills and individual decision-making abilities. Organized sports, however, tend to be adult-controlled and highly rule-structured. A perennial question for both developmental and youth sport psychologists emerges: Which games and sports are good for which individuals, and when?

The two most extensive themes of research in the study of youth sports have been motivation to participate and psychological stress (Feltz & Ewing, 1987; Gould, 1982). The evidence is still preliminary, but it suggests that children's motivation to participate in organized sports is characterized by developmental patterns. That is, having fun may be an original and abiding motive for participation, but other factors begin to emerge as important during later childhood and adolescence. Interestingly, data from a study of 103,000 young athletes in Michigan suggest that participation increases with age up to between 11 and 13 years, after which there is a sharp and steady decline (Feltz & Ewing, 1987). Studies focused on reasons for dropping out of sports programs have yielded inconclusive results, but other interests (including alternate sports) and the stress of competition have been suggested as two important variables.

The stresses of competition appear to be related to both individual and interpersonal variables: the athlete's personality makeup, the personal meaning of a specific contest or performance, fears of failure, and perceived parental pressure (Feltz, 1986; Scanlan &

Lewthwaite, 1984). Performance anxiety, for example, may vary across sports, contests, and individuals. Some interesting data on the relative stress of different activities was reported by Simon (1981). She and her colleagues at the University of Illinois studied the precompetitive anxiety of over 700 boys aged 9 to 14 in 11 different school activities. They found that playing a solo musical piece in the band was perceived as most stressful by these boys and playing with a group in band competition was the fourth most stressful activity. Wrestling and gymnastics were ranked second and third, respectively. Basketball and swimming competitions were rated as more anxiety-inducing than an academic test, but baseball, hockey, and football were reported to be less so. A softball game in physical education class was rated as least stressful, but still moderately anxiety-laden.

Youth sports enthusiasts are quick to point out that there can be both "joy and sadness in children's sports" (Martens, 1978), and that the question is not whether those activities are in the child's best interests but which ones, under what circumstances, and for which child. Contact sports, for example, may not be appropriate for children younger than 8 years old, and parents should consider their own responsibilities in helping a child choose, engage in, and enjoy a sport (N. J. Smith, R. E. Smith, & Smoll, 1983). Parents should learn about their children's expectations and motives, and, equally important, they should explore their own. Recreational programs should be examined, with particular focus on their philosophy. Fundamentally, the human rights of children should be acknowledged and embodied in youth sports programs. Those rights include the right to participate and have fun in safe surroundings, the right to be treated with dignity, and the right to try (Martens & Seefeldt, 1979).

A relevant perspective from a 7-year-old is pertinent here. His name is Sean, and he was one of 14 members of a PeeWee baseball team that I helped coach several years ago. We had fun, but we did not have a winning season; in fact, we didn't win a game. As I was driving Sean and a teammate home from their final defeat, his companion, Robbie, lamented that he felt absolutely horrible. Sean tried to reassure him with the comment, "It's just a game," but Robbie was inconsolable over being a loser. Sean then asserted that they were still winners even when they lost, and Robbie challenged that contradiction.

I then heard Sean offer the following little bit of philosophy:

> Robbie, do you know how many sperm were trying to be you? (Robbie shook his head.) Well, there were millions. I saw it on "Nova." They were all racing against you, but *you* won. Anybody who is alive won. So you're a winner and I'm a winner; everybody's a winner.

He is right, you know. And that *was* the most important competition any of us is ever going to be in.

Gender and Meaning in Sports

Human rights do not end with childhood, of course, and the recognition of children's rights has in fact lagged behind adult expressions. A timely and instructive example is the women's movement, which has been a powerful form of human rights activity in this century. I shall here focus specifically on our nascent liberation from gender stereotypes in recreation and athletics, and then comment on the fruitful integration of the women's movement with the "movement movement" (the growing popularity of recreational activity in modern cultures). Although many modern societies have made substantial progress in their recognition of women's rights, there is still a wide gap between ideals and practices. This is readily apparent in women's athletics. We are still in the beginning stage of realizing the extent to which personal lives can be unnecessarily constrained by tacit assumptions about gender, activity, and human potential.

Historically, women have been discouraged from a wide range of physical and athletic activities, usually because those activities were considered beyond their abilities, interests, or both. It was not considered feminine to be athletic, and an athletic woman was thought to be at risk of being unattractive to men (Harris, 1973). Although some of these stereotypes have begun to be eroded, there is still a need for more attention and activity on the part of feminist scholars. Greendorfer (1987, p. 339), for example, suggests that:

> Because sport participation in childhood and adolescence has implications for more full participation in various social spheres of adult life, it is time to devote more research attention to sport as a viable and natural activity for females.

Preliminary research on women's experiences in sport has strongly reinforced that recommendation (Boutilier & San Giovanni, 1983).

As Deaux (1984) noted in her review of a decade of gender research, "Many observed sex differences are not durable main effects, but rather influenced by task characteristics resulting in frequent interactions between sex of subject and sex-linkage of task" (p. 107). Different activities have different meanings, the latter being assigned on both personal and societal levels (Metheny, 1968).

In a recent study by Csizma, Wittig, and Schurr (1988), 199 male and female college students rated the masculinity–femininity and simplicity–complexity of 68 sports and activities. A second sample of 159 students rated the acceptability of males and females as participants in those sports, as well as how likely males and females were to participate in each. The results were illuminating. The 10 most feminine sports were cheerleading, balance beam, four forms of dance (ballet, aerobic, jazz, and modern), yoga, ice and figure skating, and gymnastics. In stark contrast, the 10 most masculine sports were boxing, football, wrestling, rugby, ice hockey, baseball, pole vault, shot put, riflery, and javelin.

Equally interesting were the data on the acceptability of male and female participation. The correlations were .88 and -.75, respectively, between masculinity-femininity ratings and the acceptability of female and male participation. The estimated likelihood of female and male participation in a sport was also highly correlated with its masculinity-feminity rating (r = .91 and -.79, respectively). There was no relation between gender stereotypes and the perceived simplicity or complexity of the sport, however.

One of the implications of this type of research is that we should look more closely at the meanings we assign to different types of movement, as well as at the personal attributes and abilities tacitly associated with masculinity and femininity. Only then will we begin to move closer to less sexist concepts of humanity, and only then can we begin to reexamine the messages and opportunities that we convey or prohibit in our roles as parents, teachers, and coaches.

Exercise and Health

There is now little doubt that physical activity is an important element in health and well-being. Research on the benefits of exercise and the role of recreation in human health is now voluminous (American Academy of Physical Education, 1984; Crews & Landers, 1987; Matarazzo, Weiss, Herd, Miller, & Weiss, 1984; Morgan, 1985c). Moreover, there is increasing evidence that those benefits are not entirely accounted for by the physiological challenges involved. Individual meaning and the joy of participation may be more difficult to measure than aerobic capacity, but this should not deter us from refining our understanding of human play and its complex personal and collective functions.

Moreover, we need to accelerate efforts to protect and extend the rights of all individuals to participate in stimulating and enjoyable recreational activities. More sports programs and health clubs need to be made accessible to and welcoming of individuals with different abilities and disabilities. Children, youth, adults, and elders of both sexes should have many options and opportunities to interact with and observe one another in physical recreation. Individuals with physical handicaps should be encouraged to explore a variety of activities that offer appropriate and ongoing challenges to their personal development. And finally, we need to work together toward integrating all individuals, at all levels, into a reformed socicty that respects the dignity of human embodiment in its infinitely unique forms.

Concluding Remarks

I conclude with a return to my opening remarks on mind–body dualism and our belated integration of human experience. Part of my own enthusiasm for sport psychology stems from its important role in developments that are taking place in psychology and in the world as we approach the turn of the century (Mahoney, in press). Within psychology, theories and research are beginning to offer some exciting new perspectives for conceptualizing the integrity of body and brain. Psychology cannot hope to become an adequate "science of mind" until it appreciates the inescapable embodiment of its subject matter. At a societal level, we have begun to recognize the role of recreation in both personal and cultural development. Belatedly, but still fortunately, we have begun to confront the abuse of sports for political and economic motives, and, in the process, the abuse of the individuals involved in those sports. Finally, at a planetary level, we are facing some issues that merit our collective consideration.

The Duke of Wellington is quoted as having said, "The battle of Waterloo was won on the playing fields of Eton" (Michener, 1976, p. 26). Presumably he meant that the skills and character developed in the context of youthful recreation were instrumental in deciding that military victory. Let us hope, however, that tomorrow's children will learn less about conquest and victory on their future playing fields than they learn about themselves, about one another, and about the means to peaceful and playful coexistence.

Classroom Exercises

The following are suggested classroom exercises for psychology instructors.

Exercise 1. Performance Anxiety

To demonstrate the individual experience and effects of performance anxiety, choose an in-class physical performance task. In small classes, those tasks might be a wastebasket free throw competition or a balance task—for example, the length of time a student can balance on one leg with eyes closed and face tilted toward the ceiling (take safety precautions against falls). In larger classes the task might be the length of time that a student can balance a coin on edge or the paper-and-pencil concentration task described in Exercise 2.

If possible, collect a baseline level of performance and then expose subgroups of the class to different experiences. To increase anxiety and impair later performance, a brief message about "choking under pressure" should suffice. Leith (1988), for example, found that simply telling students the following resulted in impaired performance:

> Research has shown that some people have a tendency to choke at the free throw line when shooting free throws. No one knows why some people tend to choking behavior. However, don't let that bother you. Go ahead and shoot your free throws. (p. 61)

Performance anxiety might be reduced by brief relaxation instructions, with emphasis on slow and deep breathing, or by listening to an appropriate piece of music.

If you cannot do the above demonstration with all students in the class, select a subset of volunteers. Post the performance results and invite self-reports about the experience. Then invite discussion and interpretation. If the results are "dramatically undramatic" or contrary to hypotheses, discuss the complexity of research and data interpretation, using practice effects and individual differences as illustrations of possible moderator variables.

Exercise 2. Concentration

To demonstrate the complexity of processes involved in concentration, run off copies of the 10 x 10 number matrices provided. For the simplest demonstration, you will need copies of two different forms of that Concentration Exercise for each student.

At the appropriate point in your lecture or lab, hand out copies of one form and tell students to leave them face down on their desks and to take out a pencil or pen. Tell them to begin only after you say "Go". At that time, their task is to turn the form over and look for the box with "00" in it. When they find it, they should mark through it with their pencil and then begin looking for and marking numbers "01," "02," and so on. Their goal should be to find and cross off as many numbers in sequence as they can in a two-minute interval. Caution them not to skip a number; their score will be the highest number reached in sequence. If there are no questions, say "Go" and give them exactly two minutes to perform the task.

continued

Exercise 2, continued

Ask them to put that form away (or to put some form of identification on it and turn it in). Then pass out copies of a different form of the exercise, again asking the students to keep it face down until the start signal. This time, tell them that you will be intentionally trying to distract them while they are performing. This can be done by calling out numbers to them, playing an audio or videotape excerpt from a comedian, or doing several things like these at the same time.

Calculate their changes in performance. How many did worse, better, or the same with distraction? How did they experience it? Preliminary data on this task with Olympic athletes suggest that many of them actually do better under distracting conditions. Invite a discussion on what that might mean. Invite discussion on the attentional demands of different sports (e.g., open vs. closed). Discuss possible dimensions of attention (e.g., broad/narrow, internal/external, process/outcome) and how they might influence different kinds of performance.

Exercise 3. Mental Rehearsal

Ask for a subgroup of volunteers to demonstrate the effects of mental processes on sports performance. Choose a task and collect baseline performance data. Then expose the subgroups to different experiences. The simplest contrast might be between mental practice and a "filler" (control) experience. An example of the latter would be having them listen to a brief explanation of the physics of trajectories à la Isaac Newton. For the mental practice group, invite them to relax and close their eyes. (A supine position facilitates some aspects of imagery, but this may not be possible.) Invite them to imagine approaching the task again. Emphasize what they might see, hear, feel, and smell in the situation. Then guide them through some slow-motion executions of successful performance, emphasizing a natural neuromuscular flow and the feeling of that movement.

Collect postexperimental performance data. Invite participants to discuss their experiences and their interpretation of the results.

Footnotes

[1]The following journals publish research and activity in sport psychology: *The Sport Psychologist,* the *Journal of the Philosophy of Sport,* and the *Journal of Sport and Exercise Psychology,* all published by Human Kinetics, P.O. Box 5076, Champaign, IL 61820; *The International Journal of Sport Psychology,* published by Edizioni Luigi Pozzi, Via Panama, 68, Rome, Italy 00198; the *Journal of Sport Behavior,* published by the Department of Health, Physical

Education and Leisure Services, University of South Alabama, Mobile, AL 36688; *Research Quarterly for Exercise and Sport,* published by the American Alliance for Health, Physical Education, Recreation, and Dance, 1900 Association Drive, Reston, VA 22091; *Physician and Sportsmedicine,* published by McGraw-Hill Book Company, 1221 Avenue of the Americas, New York, NY 10020; *Medicine and Science in Sports and Exercise,* published by Williams and Wilkins, 428 E. Preston St., Baltimore, MD 21202; and the *Journal of Sports Medicine and Physical Fitness,* published by Edizioni Minerva Medica (Corso Bramante 83-85, Torino, Italy 10126) and distributed by J.B. Lippincott Company, East Washington Square, Philadelphia, PA 19105.

[2]For more information on these issues, contact the Association for the Advancement of Applied Sport Psychology (AAASP), John M. Silva, Department of Physical Education, 203 Fetzer 468–A, University of North Carolina, Chapel Hill, NC 27514. Information about the USOC Sport Psychology Registry can be obtained from the U.S. Olympic Committee Sports Medicine Council, 1750 E. Boulder St., Colorado Springs, CO 80909. For information about the North American Society for the Psychology of Sport and Physical Activity (NASPSPA), write Deborah L. Feltz, Youth Sports Institute, Michigan State University, East Lansing, MI 48824. Information on the American Psychological Association's Division (47) of Exercise and Sport Psychology can be obtained from Daniel M. Landers, Exercise and Sports Research Institute, Arizona State University, Tempe, AZ 85281.

References

American Academy of Physical Education. (1984). *Exercise and health.* Champaign, IL: Human Kinetics.

Bandura, A. (1977). Self-efficacy: Toward a unifying theory of behavioral change. *Psychological Review, 84,* 191–215.

Bandura, A. (1982). Self-efficacy in human agency. *American Psychologist, 37,* 122–147.

Bandura, A. (1986). *Social foundations of thought and action: A social cognitive theory.* Englewood Cliffs, NJ: Prentice-Hall.

Boutilier, M., & San Giovanni, L. (Eds.). (1983). *The sporting woman.* Champaign, IL: Human Kinetics.

Bretherton, I. (1984). *Symbolic play: The development of social understanding.* New York: Academic Press.

Burton, D. (1988). Do anxious swimmers swim slower? Reexamining the elusive anxiety-performance relationship. *Journal of Sport and Exercise Psychology, 10,* 45–61.

Coakley, J. J. (1980). Play, games, and sport: Developmental implications for young people. *Journal of Sport Behavior, 3,* 99–118.

Corbin, C. B. (1972). Mental practice. In W. P. Morgan (Ed.), *Ergogenic aids and muscular performance* (pp. 94–118). New York: Academic Press.

Crews, D. J., & Landers, D. M. (1987). A meta-analytic review of aerobic fitness and reactivity to psychosocial stressors. *Medicine and Science in Sports and Exercise, 19,* S114–S120.

Csikszentmihalyi, M. (1975). *Beyond boredom and anxiety: The experience of games in work and play.* San Francisco: Jossey-Bass.

Csikszentmihalyi, M., & Csikszentmihalyi, I. S. (Eds.). (1988). *Optimal experience: Psychological studies of flow in consciousness.* Cambridge: Cambridge University Press.
Csizma, K. A., Wittig, A. F., & Schurr, K. T. (1988). Sports stereotypes and gender. *Journal of Sport and Exercise Psychology, 10,* 62-74.
Danish, S. J., & Hale, B. D. (1981). Toward an understanding of the practice of sport psychology. *Journal of Sport Psychology, 3,* 90-99.
Deaux, K. (1984). From individual differences to social categories: Analysis of a decade's research on gender. *American Psychologist, 39,* 105-116.
Dishman, R. K., Ickes, W., & Morgan, W. P. (1980). Self-motivation and adherence to habitual physical activity. *Journal of Applied Social Psychology, 10,* 115-132.
Epstein, M. L. (1980). The relationship of mental imagery and mental rehearsal to performance on a motor task. *Journal of Sport Psychology, 2,* 211-220.
Fein, G. G. (1981). Pretend play in childhood: An integrative review. *Child Development, 52,* 1095-1118.
Feltz, D. L. (1986). The relevance of youth sports for clinical child psychology. *The Clinical Psychologist, 39,* 74-77.
Feltz, D. L. (1988). Self-confidence and sports performance. In K. B. Pandolf (Ed.), *Exercise and sport sciences review, 16,* 423-457.
Feltz, D. L., & Ewing, M. E. (1987). Psychological characteristics of elite young athletes. *Medicine and Science in Sports and Exercise, 19,* S98-S104.
Feltz, D. L., & Landers, D. M. (1983). The effects of mental practice on motor skill learning and performance: A meta-analysis. *Journal of Sport Psychology, 5,* 25-27.
Fenz, W. D. (1988). Learning to anticipate stressful events. *Journal of Sport and Exercise Psychology, 10,* 223-228.
Fisher, A. C. (1976). In search of the albatross. In A. C. Fisher (Ed.), *Psychology of sport* (pp. 400-407). Palo Alto, CA: Mayfield.
Fisher, A. C. (1984). New directions in sport personality research. In J. M. Silva & R. S. Weinberg (Eds.), *Psychological foundations of sport* (pp. 70-80). Champaign, IL: Human Kinetics.
Gauron, E. F. (1984). *Mental training for peak performance.* Lansing, NY: Sport Science Associates.
Gentile, A. M. (1972). A working model of skill acquisition with application to teaching. *Quest, 17,* 3-23.
Gould, D. (1982). Sport psychology in the 1980s: Status, direction, and challenge in youth sports research. *Journal of Sport Psychology, 4,* 203-218.
Gould, D., Weiss, M., & Weinberg, R. (1981). Psychological characteristics of successful and nonsuccessful Big Ten wrestlers. *Journal of Sport Psychology, 3,* 69-81.
Greendorfer, S. L. (1987). Gender bias in theoretical perspectives: The case of female socialization into sport. *Psychology of Women Quarterly, 11,* 327-340.
Hale, B. D. (1982). The effects of internal and external imagery on muscular and ocular concomitants. *Journal of Sport Psychology, 4,* 379-387.
Hall, H. K., & Byrne, A. T. J. (1988). Goal setting in sport: Clarifying recent anomalies. *Journal of Sport and Exercise Psychology, 10,* 184-198.

Harris, D. V. (1973). *Involvement in sport: A somatopsychic rationale for physical activity.* Philadelphia, PA: Lea & Febiger.

Harris, D. V., & Harris, B. L. (1984). *The athlete's guide to sports psychology: Mental skills for physical people.* Champaign, IL: Leisure Press.

Harris, D. V., & Robinson, W. J. (1986). The effects of skill level of EMG activity during internal and external imagery. *Journal of Sport Psychology, 8,* 105–111.

Harrison, R. P., & Feltz, D. L. (1979). The professionalization of sport psychology: Legal considerations. *Journal of Sport Psychology, 1,* 182–190.

Hatfield, B. D., & Landers, D. M. (1987). Psychophysiology in exercise and sport research: An overview. *Exercise and Sport Sciences Review, 15,* 351–387.

Hatfield, B. D., Landers, D. M., & Ray, W. J. (1987). Cardiovascular-CNS interactions during a self-paced, intentional attentive state: Elite marksmanship performance. *Psychophysiology, 24,* 542–549.

Hemery, D. (1986). *Sporting excellence: A study of sport's highest achievers.* Champaign, IL: Human Kinetics.

Heyman, S. R. (1984). The development of models for sport psychology: Examining the USOC guidelines. *Journal of Sport Psychology, 6,* 125–132.

Heyman, S. R. (1986). Psychological problem patterns found with athletes. *The Clinical Psychologist, 39,* 68–71.

Highlen, P. S., & Bennett, B. B. (1979). Psychological characteristics of successful and nonsuccessful elite wrestlers: An exploratory study. *Journal of Sport Psychology, 1,* 123–137.

Jerome, J. (1980). *The sweet spot in time.* New York: Summit.

Kane, J. E. (1978). Personality research: The current controversy and implications for sports studies. In W. F. Straub (Ed.), *Sport psychology: An analysis of athlete behavior* (pp. 228–240). Ithaca, NY: Mouvement Publications.

Kroll, W., & Lewis, G. (1970). America's first sport psychologist. *Quest, 13,* 1–4.

Landers, D. M., Christina, R. W., Hatfield, B. D., Daniels, F. S., & Doyle, L. A. (1980). Moving competitive shooting into the scientists' lab. *American Rifleman, 128,* 36–37, 76–77.

Lee, C., & Owen, N. (1986). Self-help books in behavioural sport psychology. *Behaviour Change, 3,* 127–134.

Leith, L. M. (1988). Choking in sports: Are we our own worst enemies? *International Journal of Sport Psychology, 19,* 59–64.

Leonard, G. (1974). *The ultimate athlete.* New York: Viking.

Leslie, A. M. (1987). Pretense and representation: The origins of "theory of mind." *Psychological Review, 94,* 412–426.

Locke, E. A., & Latham, G. P. (1985). The application of goal setting to sports. *Journal of Sport Psychology, 7,* 205–222.

Mahoney, M. J. (1979). Cognitive skills and athletic performance. In P. C. Kendall & S. D. Hollon (Eds.), *Cognitive-behavioral interventions: Theory, research, and procedures* (pp. 423–443). New York: Academic Press.

Mahoney, M. J. (1988). *Performance skills series* (Audiocassettes). Goleta, CA: Health Science Systems.

Mahoney, M. J. (in press). *Human change processes: Notes on the facilitation of personal development.* New York: Basic Books.

Mahoney, M. J., & Avener, M. (1977). Psychology of the elite athlete: An exploratory study. *Cognitive Therapy and Research, 1,* 135–141.
Mahoney M. J., Gabriel, T. J., & Perkins, T. S. (1987). Psychological skills and exceptional athletic performance. *The Sport Psychologist, 1,* 181–199.
Mahoney, M. J., & Meyers, A. W. (1989). Anxiety and athletic performance: Traditional and cognitive-developmental perspectives. In D. Hackfort & C. D. Spielberger (Eds.), *Anxiety in sports: An international perspective* (pp. 77–94). Washington, DC: Hemisphere.
Martens, R. (1975). The paradigmatic crises in American sport personology. *Sportwissenschaft, 5,* 9–24.
Martens, R. (1978). *Joy and sadness in children's sports.* Champaign, IL: Human Kinetics.
Martens, R. (1987). *Coaches' guide to sport psychology.* Champaign, IL: Human Kinetics.
Martens, R., & Seefeldt, V. (1979). *Guidelines for children's sports.* Washington, DC: American Alliance for Health, Physical Education, Recreation & Dance.
Maslow, A. H. (1968). *Toward a psychology of being.* Princeton, NJ: Van Nostrand Reinhold.
Matarazzo, J. D., Weiss, S. M., Herd, J. A., Miller, N. E., & Weiss, S. M. (Eds.). (1984). *Behavioral health: A handbook of health enhancement and disease prevention.* New York: Wiley.
May, J. R. (1986). Sport psychology: Should psychologists become involved? *The Clinical Psychologist, 39,* 77–81.
McFarland, D. (Ed.). (1987). *The Oxford companion to animal behaviour.* Oxford: Oxford University Press.
McNair, D. M., Lorr, M., & Droppleman, L. F. (1971). *The profile of mood states* (1st ed.). San Diego, CA: Educational and Industrial Testing Service.
Metheny, E. (1968). *Movement and meaning.* New York: McGraw-Hill.
Michener, J. A. (1976). *Sports in America.* New York: Fawcett.
Morgan, W. J., & Meier, K. V. (Eds.). (1988). *Philosophic inquiry in sport.* Champaign, IL: Human Kinetics.
Morgan, W. P. (1978). Sport personology: The credulous, skeptical argument in perspective. In W. F. Straub (Ed.), *Sport psychology: An analysis of athlete behavior* (pp. 218–227). Ithaca, NY: Mouvement Publications.
Morgan, W. P. (1980). The trait psychology controversy. *Research Quarterly for Exercise and Sport, 51,* 50–76.
Morgan, W. P. (1985a). Selected psychological factors limiting performance: A mental health model. In D. H. Clarke & H. M. Eckert (Eds.), *Limits of human performance* (pp. 70–80). Champaign, IL: Human Kinetics.
Morgan, W. P. (1985b). Psychogenic factors and exercise metabolism: A review. *Medicine and Science in Sports and Exercise, 17,* 309–316.
Morgan, W. P. (1985c). Affective beneficence of vigorous physical activity. *Medicine and Science in Sports and Exercise, 17,* 94–100.
Morgan, W. P., Brown, D. R., Raglin, J. S., O'Connor, P. J., & Ellickson, K. A. (1987). Psychological monitoring of overtraining and staleness. *British Journal of Sports Medicine, 21,* 107–114.
Morgan, W. P., & Pollock, M. L. (1977). Psychologic characterization of the

elite distance runner. *Annals of the New York Academy of Science, 301,* 382–403.

Murphy, M., & White, R. (1978). *The psychic side of sports.* Reading, MA: Addison-Wesley.

Neiss, R. (1988). Reconceptualizing arousal: Psychobiological states in motor performance. *Psychological Bulletin, 103,* 345–366.

Nideffer, R. M. (1976), *The inner athlete: Mind plus muscle for winning.* New York: Crowell.

Ogilvie, B. C. (1968). Psychological consistencies within the personality of high-level competitors. *Journal of the American Medical Association, 205,* 156–162.

Orlick, T. (1980). *In pursuit of excellence.* Ottawa, Ontario (Canada): Coaching Association of Canada.

Oxendine, J. B. (1970). Emotional arousal and motor performance. *Quest, 13,* 23–32.

Passer, M. W. (1984). Competitive trait anxiety in children and adolescents. In J. M. Silva & R. S. Weinberg (Eds.), *Psychological foundations of sport* (pp. 130–144). Champaign, IL: Human Kinetics.

Piaget, J. (1962). *Play, dreams and imitation in childhood.* New York: Norton.

Richardson, A. (1967a). Mental practice: A review and discussion. Part I. *Research Quarterly, 38,* 95–107.

Richardson, A. (1967b). Mental practice: A review and discussion. Part II. *Research Quarterly, 38,* 263–273.

Roberts, G. C. (1984). Toward a new theory of motivation in sport: The role of perceived ability. In J. M. Silva & R. S. Weinberg (Eds.), *Psychological foundations of sport* (pp. 214–228). Champaign, IL: Human Kinetics.

Rosen, G. M. (1987). Self-help treatment books and the commercialization of psychotherapy. *American Psychologist, 42,* 46–51.

Ryan, E. D. (1976). The questions we ask and the decisions we make. In A. C. Fisher (Ed.), *Psychology of sport* (pp. 408–414). Palo Alto, CA: Mayfield.

Sadalla, E. K., Linder, D. E., & Jenkins, B. A. (1988). Sport preference: A self-presentational analysis. *Journal of Sport and Exercise Psychology, 10,* 214–222.

Scanlan, T. K., & Lewthwaite, R. (1984). Social psychological aspects of competition for male youth sport participants: I. Predictors of competitive stress. *Journal of Sport Psychology,* pp. 208–226.

Segrave, J., & Chu, D. (Eds.). (1981). *Olympism.* Champaign, IL: Human Kinetics.

Shelton, T. O., & Mahoney, M. J. (1978). The content and effect of "psyching-up" strategies in weightlifters. *Cognitive Therapy and Research, 2,* 275–284.

Silva, J. M. (1984). Personality and sport performance: Controversy and challenge. In J. M. Silva & R. S. Weinberg (Eds.), *Psychological foundations of sport* (pp. 59–69). Champaign, IL: Human Kinetics.

Simon, J. (1981). Stress in kids' sports. *Sports Line, 3*(1), 5–7.

Smith, N. J., Smith, R. E., & Smoll, F. L. (1983). *Kidsports: A survival guide for parents.* Reading, MA: Addison-Wesley.

Smith, R. E. (1986). Toward a cognitive-affective model of athletic burnout. *Journal of Sport Psychology, 8,* 36–50.

Sonstroem, R. J. (1984). An overview of anxiety in sport. In J. M. Silva &

R. S. Weinberg (Eds.), *Psychological foundations of sport* (pp. 104–117). Champaign, IL: Human Kinetics.

Suinn, R. M. (1985). Imagery rehearsal applications to performance enhancememt. *The Behavior Therapist, 8,* 155–159.

Syer, J., & Connolly, C. (1984). *Sporting body, sporting mind: An athlete's guide to mental training.* Cambridge: Cambridge University Press.

Triplett, N. (1987). The dynamogenic factors in pacemaking and competition. *American Journal of Psychology, 9,* 507–553.

Tutko, T., & Tosi, U. (1976). *Sports psyching: Playing your best game all of the time.* Los Angeles: J. P. Tarcher.

Underwood, C. (1984). *The student athlete: Eligibility and academic integrity.* East Lansing, MI: Michigan State University Press.

Unesthal, L. E. (1980). *Better sport by inner mental training.* Orebro, Sweden: Veje.

Vanek, M., & Cratty, B. J. (1970). *Psychology and the superior athlete.* London: Collier-Macmillan.

Vealey, R. S. (1986). Conceptualization of sport-confidence and competitive orientation: Preliminary investigation and instrument development. *Journal of Sport Psychology, 8,* 221–246.

Waicukauski, R. J. (1982). The regulation of academic standards in intercollegiate athletics. In R. J. Waicukauski (Ed.), *Law and amateur sports* (pp. 161–181). Bloomington, IN: Indiana University Press.

Waitley, D. (1980). *The winner's edge.* New York: Berkley Publishing Corp.

Weinberg, R. S. (1984a). The relationship between extrinsic rewards and instrinsic motivation in sport. In J. M. Silva & R. S. Weinberg (Eds.), *Psychological foundations of sport* (pp. 177–187). Champaign, IL: Human Kinetics.

Weinberg, R. S. (1984b). Mental preparation strategies. In J. M. Silva & R. S. Weinberg (Eds.), *Psychological foundations of sport* (pp. 145–156). Champaign, IL: Human Kinetics.

Weiss, P. (1969). *Sport: A philosophic inquiry.* Carbondale, IL: Southern Illinois University Press.

Yerkes, R. M., & Dodson, J. D. (1908). The relationship of strength of stimulus in rapidity of habit formation. *Journal of Comparative Neurology and Psychology, 18,* 459–482.

RICHARD E. MAYER

TEACHING FOR THINKING: RESEARCH ON THE TEACHABILITY OF THINKING SKILLS

Richard E. Mayer loves problems. During the past 20 years, he has been studying how people solve math problems, like how to calculate the cost of a tankful of gasoline; science problems, like how to improve the efficiency of a radar system; and computer programming problems, like how to write a BASIC program that sorts numbers into even and odd categories. In particular, he has focused on how we can help people to become better problem solvers.

Mayer earned a BA degree (with honors) from Miami University (Oxford, Ohio) in 1969 and a PhD degree from the University of Michigan (Ann Arbor) in 1973. After spending two years as a visiting assistant professor of psychology at Indiana University from 1973 to 1975, Mayer settled in at the University of California at Santa Barbara, where he is now department chair and professor of psychology.

Mayer is the author, coauthor, or editor of a dozen books, including *The Promise of Cognitive Psychology* (1981, published by W.H. Freeman), *Thinking, Problem Solving, Cognition* (1983, published by W.H. Freeman), *Educational Psychology: A Cognitive Approach* (1987, published by Little, Brown and Company), and *Teaching and Learning Computer Programming* (1988, published by Lawrence Erlbaum Associates). He is the author or coauthor of over 100 publications in educational and cognitive psychology, including over 30 research articles in the *Journal of Educational Psychology*. His research on human learning and problem solving has been supported by a series of seven grants from the National Science Foundation and two grants from the National Institute of Education.

Mayer was elected to serve as Secretary-Treasurer of Division 15 of the American Psychological Association, Secretary of Division C of the American Educational Research Association, and on the Executive Board of the Society for Computers in Psychology. From 1984 to 1988 he served as the Editor of the *Educational Psychologist,* and from 1983 to 1987 he served as Coeditor of *Instructional Science.* Currently he serves on the Editorial Boards of the *Journal of Educational Psychology, Journal of Educational Computing Research, Instructional Science, Educational Technology Review and Development, Educational Psychologist,* and *Educational Psychology Review.* He is also serving a six-year term on the Publications and Communications Board of the American Psychological Association and has served for eight years as a school board member in the Goleta Union School District.

RICHARD E. MAYER

TEACHING FOR THINKING: RESEARCH ON THE TEACHABILITY OF THINKING SKILLS

What does it mean to teach for thinking? Can the way that we teach affect the way that our students think? Can education help students to improve their thinking? If so, how, and how much? These are the kinds of questions that motivate this chapter.

My purpose is to explore the idea that students can be taught in ways that will help them to become better thinkers. By better thinkers, I mean students who are better able to take what they learn and use it successfully in new situations. These students are better able to transfer knowledge that helps them solve previously unencountered problems.

I examine three exemplary thinking-skills programs carried out through our research laboratory in Santa Barbara that demonstrate techniques for improving students' skills in the domains of scientific thinking, mathematical thinking, and computer programming. In structure training, students learn how to outline sections of their science textbooks based on typical ways of organizing scientific text. In representation training, students learn how to translate sentences from mathematical word problems into concrete diagrams. In conceptual model training, students learn how to describe what goes on

The research descriptions in sections 2, 3, and 4 are based on doctoral dissertations by Cook (1982), Lewis (1989), and Bayman (1983), respectively. More complete discussion of research on thinking and thinking skills can be found in Mayer (1983, 1987a).

inside the computer for several BASIC computer programming statements. Each training program results in the improvement of students' abilities to transfer what they have learned to new problem-solving tasks. These successful programs of teaching for thinking are based on (a) teaching small component skills rather than viewing intellectual performance as a single monolithic ability; (b) asking students to model the process of problem solving rather than asking them only to produce the correct answer; and (c) embedding instruction within specific subject domains rather than isolating instruction in thinking as a separate, domain-free topic.

What is Teaching for Thinking?

Suppose we ask a student to read a passage about hearing such as the one found in the top left portion of Table 1. Then, we ask the student to answer retention questions that focus on material that was explicitly presented in the passage and to answer transfer questions that require the student to apply what was presented creatively to new situations. For example, based on the hearing passage, the middle portion of the first row of Table 1 lists a retention problem, and the right top portion of Table 1 lists a transfer problem.

Next, suppose we teach a student to solve two-step word problems such as those shown in the left portion of the second row in Table 1. Following instruction, we test the student on retention problems that are very similar to those given during instruction, such as similarly worded two-step problems, and on transfer problems that go beyond what was explicitly taught, such as three-step problems. Examples are shown in the middle and right portions of the second row of Table 1, respectively.

Finally, suppose we teach a student to comprehend and generate each of 10 elementary BASIC programming statements such as INPUT, LET, PRINT, and so on. After instruction, we test the student on retention problems that are very similar to those given during instruction, such as generating single statements, and on transfer problems, such as generating and comprehending short programs that go beyond what was explicitly taught. Examples of taught material, retention questions, and transfer questions are shown in the left, middle, and right portions of the third row of Table 1, respectively.

Table 2 lists three possible learning outcomes for any of these examples. First, the student may perform poorly on retention and on transfer. This performance, labeled *no learning* in Table 2, would suggest that the student did not learn very much. Second, the student may perform well on retention but poorly on transfer. This student would seem to have learned what was taught but to be unable to ap-

Table 1
Examples of Retention and Transfer Problems in Three Subject Domains

Taught material	Retention problem	Transfer problem
Hearing can be described in five separate stages. First sound waves are captured by the external portion of the ear. The outer ear's function is to focus or concentrate these sound waves. During the second stage, the sound waves travel down the auditory canal (a tube embedded in the bones of the skull) . . .	A tube embedded in the bones of the skull is called ______________.	A child cannot hear sounds in her left ear. List all the possible reasons for this you can think of.
Tom is 35 years old. Zino is 7 years older than Tom. How old will Zino be in 10 years?	Mary is 12 years old. Her sister is 6 years older than her. How old will Mary's sister be in 2 years?	Alfredo is 25 years old. Pedro is 7 years younger than Alfredo, and Dennis is 3 years older than Pedro. How old will Dennis be in 8 years?
Assume that you type in LET A = 1 and press the RETURN key. The value, 1, will be stored in variable A. Assume that you type in LET B = 2 and press the RETURN key. The value, 2, will be stored in variable B. Finally, assume that you type in LET C = A + B and press the RETURN key. The value, 3, will be stored in variable C . . .	Which of the following is not a legal statement? LET A = 1 LET B = 2 LET A + B = C	What number will appear on the screen after you run the following program? LET X = 5 LET Y = X LET Y = X + Y PRINT

ply what was learned to new situations. In Table 2, this kind of learning outcome is labeled *nonmeaningful learning.* Finally, the student may perform well on retention and on transfer, indicating that the student learned the material and was able to apply what was learned to new situations. Table 2 refers to this outcome as *meaningful learning* (Mayer, 1984, 1987c).

Table 2
Three Possible Learning Outcomes

Learning outcome	Retention performance	Transfer performance
No learning	Poor	Poor
Nonmeaningful learning	Good	Poor
Meaningful learning	Good	Good

Note. Adapted from Mayer (1984).

The analysis summarized in Table 2 is intended only as an illustration and requires a great deal of additional research and theory-based clarification. However, it does provide a simple way of defining meaningful learning; namely, *meaningful learning* is learning that results in the transfer of learned material to new situations. The goal of teaching for thinking is to create meaningful learning, the third kind of learning outcome listed in Table 2. For the purpose of this paper, we can view teaching for thinking as an attempt to teach domain-specific material in a way that enables students to use what they learn to solve transfer problems.

How Can We Teach for Thinking?

As an introduction to the issues involved in teaching for thinking, let me ask you to imagine that you are responsible for developing an educational program that will improve the way that students think. Assume that you have both vast economic resources and commitments from the nation's school systems to implement your program faithfully. What would you do?

The research literature indicates that previous attempts to teach students to become better thinkers have not always turned out to be well-documented successes (Detterman & Sternberg, 1982; Mayer, 1987a, 1987b; Nickerson, Perkins, & Smith, 1985; Segal, Chipman, & Glaser, 1985). From the Latin School movement's attempts to teach "proper habits of mind" in previous centuries to more modern attempts to stimulate cognitive development through Project Head Start, the search for solid evidence of teaching students to think has been elusive and has often been disappointing (Mayer, 1987a, 1987b). In fact, one of the most persistent research findings in the problem-solving literature is that people who learn how to solve one kind of problem rarely are able to transfer what they have learned to solve new kinds of problems (Mayer, 1983).

In spite of this disappointing history, however, current research and theory in cognitive psychology may provide some answers that were not available for previous thinking-skills projects. In particular, to develop a program of teaching for thinking, one must answer several questions concerning what should be taught, how it should be taught, and where it should be taught. These issues are summarized in Table 3.

Table 3
Three Issues Underlying Teaching for Thinking

Issue	Alternatives
1. What to teach	Thinking as a single intellectual ability versus thinking as a collection of smaller component skills
2. How to teach	Focus on product through rewarding correct answers versus focus on processes that the student learns to model
3. Where to teach	In general, domain-independent courses versus within existing, specific subject areas

The first question examines what should be taught: Should we view thinking as a single, unitary intellectual ability or as a collection of smaller component skills? In this paper, I break down the content of a problem-solving program into a collection of small component skills, such as techniques for how to outline scientific text, how to represent sentences from story problems in diagram form, or how to relate lines of computer programming code to a concrete model of the computer.

The second question concerns how to teach: Should we focus on product or process? That is, should we focus on getting the right answers in problem solving or on the methods and strategies for problem solving? This paper opts for the second approach of helping students to model the process by which an expert thinks about solving scientific, mathematical, or programming problems.

The third question focuses on where thinking should be taught: Is it better to teach thinking skills in domain-independent, general problem-solving courses or to integrate thinking-skills instruction within existing subject domains? The research literature on the transfer of problem-solving skills prompts me to focus on the second option. Instead of examining the teaching of general thinking skills, I will examine teaching for thinking within three specific domains: science, mathematics, and computer programming.

In summary, a comparison of the features of successful and unsuccessful (or undocumented) thinking-skills programs suggests three conditions for success: a focus on teaching component skills, the use of modeling techniques that emphasize the problem-solving process, and the embedding of instruction within existing subject domains (Mayer, 1987a, 1987b).

Teaching for Scientific Thinking

Issue

As an example, consider the following scenario. Some students are taking their first college science course at a junior college. The students are relatively inexperienced in reading college-level science textbooks and lack strong backgrounds in science. They devote a great deal of time and energy to the course, and they read every word of their textbooks. However, when the teacher posts the examination grades, it is clear that the students are not passing the course. Some students are able to remember facts from the textbook but have difficulty applying this information to solve new problems, and other students even have difficulty remembering facts from the textbook.

What is your diagnosis? Based on the analysis given in Table 2, the students appear to show learning outcomes that correspond to the no learning or nonmeaningful learning categories. The students may have excellent strategies for reading narrative text, but they seem to lack appropriate strategies for reading expository text. What is your prescription for remedying this problem? What we need is a method of teaching the students to read their science textbooks in a way that results in meaningful learning—that is, in a way that allows them to transfer what they have learned to new problems.

Structure Training

What can we do to help science students become more effective learners and thinkers? Cook (1982; Cook & Mayer, 1988) devised a structure training program to help students improve their comprehension of scientific text. The training takes abut 9 hours and consists of two major objectives. The first objective is to teach students how to distinguish among various text structures commonly found in science text. Table 4 describes and exemplifies several of the text structures often used in science textbooks, including generalization, enumeration, and sequence. Students then learn to identify the text structure of paragraphs from their own science textbooks.

The second objective is to teach students how to outline passages of each type of text structure. For example, for generalization passages, students write the main assertion followed by the supporting evidence; for sequence passages, they name and describe each step in the process; and for enumeration passages, they list the main topic and the subtopics. The worksheet students use to learn about outlining generalization passages is summarized in Table 5.

Each session involves several episodes of presenting students with a paragraph from their own textbook and asking students to identify the paragraph's text structure and to outline the paragraph. Students receive practice with feedback, and the instructor models how to identify and outline paragraphs.

As you can see, Cook's structure training is consistent with the three aspects of successful programs described in the first section of this paper. First, the training focuses on small component skills, namely, on strategies for how to recognize and outline specific kinds of text structures. Second, the training emphasizes process, namely, the active modeling of reading comprehension techniques. Third, the training is embedded within a specific subject area, namely, reading science textbooks.

Evaluation of Structure Training

Does structure training work? To answer this question, Cook provided structure training to a group of introductory chemistry students at a junior college. Before training, the students took a pretest in which they read biology passages and were then asked to recall and answer questions about the passages. After training, the students took an equivalent posttest. Control students from the same course took the pretest and posttest without training during the intervening period.

The pretest-to-posttest changes in recall and question answering performance of the structure-trained and control groups are summarized in Figure 1. On the pretest, both groups scored at about the same level for each measure of performance: recalling important information, recalling unimportant information, correctly answering retention questions, and correctly answering transfer questions. However, as you can see in Figure 1, the trained group showed a large

Table 4
Examples of Text Structures Used in Science Textbooks

Description	Example
Generalization	
Passage always has a main idea. Most of the other sentences in the passage try to provide evidence for the main idea by either clarifying or extending. Some sentences explain the main idea by using examples or illustrations; these tend to *clarify* the main idea. Other sentences explain the main idea in more detail; these *extend* the main idea.	Irritability is defined as an organism's capacity to respond to conditions outside itself. An organism responds to a stimulus from the environment. The stimulus may be light, temperature, water, sound, the presence of a chemical substance or a threat to life. The organism's response is the way it reacts to stimulus. For example, a plant may have a growth response. This happens when a root pushes toward water or a stem grows unevenly and bends toward light.
Enumeration	
List of facts one after other. There are two general kinds of enumeration passages: *specified*—lists the facts by numbering them; *unspecified*—lists facts in paragraph form, with each fact stated in one or more sentences.	There are four general properties of solids: (1) Tenacity is a measure of a solid's resistance to being pulled apart. (2) Hardness is a measure of a substance's ability to scratch another substance. (3) Malleability refers to a solid's ability to be hammered or rolled into thin sheets. (4) Ductility is the ability to be drawn out in the form of wires.

Sequence	
Describe a continuous and connected series of events or the steps in a process. Examples of sequences include changes as the result of growth, a biological process, steps in an experiment, or the evolution of some event.	Hearing can be described in five separate stages. First, sound waves are captured by the external portion of the ear. The outer ear's function is to focus or concentrate these sound waves. During the second stage, the sound waves travel down the auditory canal (a tube embedded in the bones of the skull) and strike the tympanic membrane or eardrum. The third stage occurs when the vibrations of the eardrum begin a series of similar vibrations in several small bones. These vibrations are then transmitted to the inner ear called the cochlea during the fourth stage. At this point the vibrations are turned into neural impulses that are sent to the brain. The fifth and final stage of the hearing process represents the brain's interpretation of the sound patterns.

Note. Adapted from Cook and Mayer (1988) with permission.

Table 5
Example Worksheet for Structure Training

STEP 1: Identify the generalization (main idea)

List and define key words in the generalization

Word	Definition

Restate the generalization in your own words

STEP 2: What kind of support is there for the generalization?
Does it use examples, illustrations?
Does it extend or clarify the generalization?

Supporting evidence	Relation to generalization

Note. This worksheet is for generalization passages. Adapted from Cook and Mayer (1988).

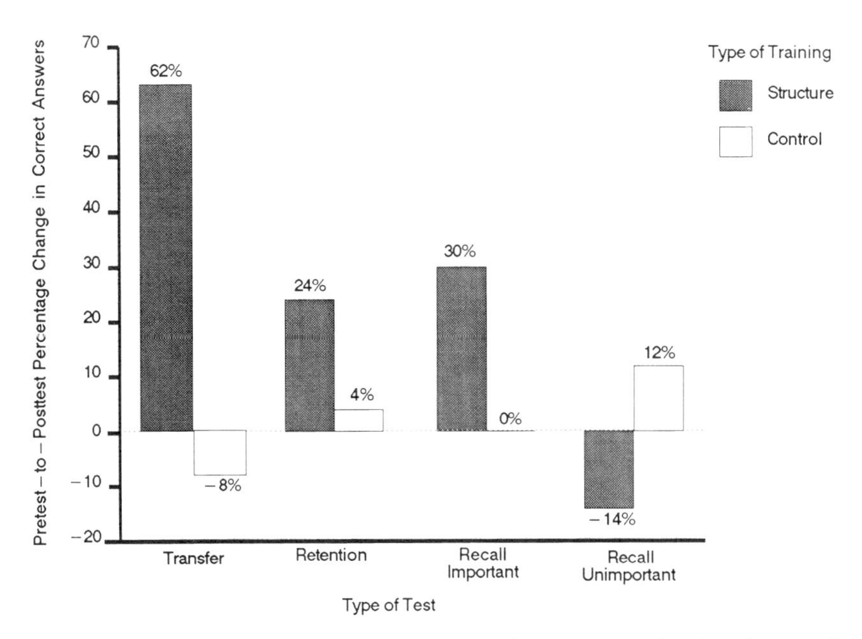

Figure 1. Pretest-to-posttest changes of structure trained and control groups. Adapted from Cook and Mayer (1988).

pretest-to-posttest gain in recalling important information and in answering transfer questions, whereas the control group did not.

These results are consistent with the idea that structure training helps students focus on important information and organize the information in a way that allows for successful transfer. The trained group's pattern of performance demonstrated a meaningful learning outcome, whereas the control group's performance more closely corresponded to nonmeaningful learning.

Although the results were positive, it is important to note the conditions under which the results were achieved. First, if we had focused only on overall amount recalled or overall amount retained, we would not have concluded that structure training had an effect. The effects of structure training are most obvious when we look at transfer performance and at the recall of important information. Second, if our subjects had been experienced readers of scientific text, our instructional training probably would not have been successful. This is so because experienced science readers are likely to already have developed appropriate reading comprehension strategies. The effects of structure training are likely to be most pronounced for students who are adequate readers but who lack domain-specific experience in reading scientific text.

Teaching for Mathematical Thinking

Issue

As a second example, suppose we walked into a mathematics classroom and asked the students to solve some problems like those in Table 6. These are called *two-step problems* because each problem requires two mathematical computations, such as adding .05 to 1.13 and multiplying the result by 5. The problem on the top of Table 6 is called *consistent* because the keyword in the problem (i.e., *more*) is consistent with the required arithmetic operation (i.e., addition), whereas the problem on the bottom is called *inconsistent* because the keyword in the problem (i.e., *less*) conflicts with the required operation (i.e., addition).

Although both problems require the same arithmetic operations, suppose we find that students are far more likely to make errors on the inconsistent problems than on the consistent problems. A particularly difficult aspect of these problems is that they contain relational statements, that is, sentences that assert a quantitative relationship between two variables such as the second sentence in each problem in Table 6 (Mayer, 1982). For example, instead of adding 1.13 and .05 in the second problem, a sizeable proportion of students subtract .05 from 1.13. Even though our students can solve computational problems such as $(1.13 + .05) \times 5 =$ ____, they are often unable to solve corresponding word problems such as the second problem in Table 6. This pattern of performance was obtained in a study by Lewis and Mayer (1987).

Table 6
Examples of Word Problems Used in Mathematics Education

Problem type	Example
Consistent two-step	At ARCO gas sells for $1.13 per gallon. Gas at Chevron is 5 cents more per gallon than gas at ARCO. How much do 5 gallons of gas cost at Chevron?
Inconsistent two-step	At ARCO gas sells for $1.13 per gallon. This is 5 cents less per gallon than gas at Chevron. How much do 5 gallons of gas cost at Chevron?

Note. Adapted from Lewis & Mayer (1987).

What kinds of knowledge do our students need to solve word problems like the gasoline problem in Table 6? Table 7 provides a summary of how mathematical problem solving can be broken down into two major phases: representation, in which the student creates a mental representation of the problem; and solution, in which the student establishes and carries out a plan for appropriate mathematical operations such as addition and multiplication (Mayer, 1985b; Mayer, Larkin, & Kadane, 1984). For example, to represent the gasoline problem, the student must translate each sentence into other forms such as diagrams or equations and must then integrate this information into a coherent representation; for problem solution, the student must devise a plan such as finding the cost per gallon and finding the total cost and must execute the plan by adding .05 and 1.13 and by multiplying 1.18 by 5.

Table 7
Types of Knowledge Required to Solve Word Problems

Problem: At ARCO gas sells for $1.13 per gallon. This is 5 cents less per gallon than gas at Chevron. How much do 5 gallons of gas cost at Chevron?

Step	Knowledge	Example from gasoline problem
Representation	Linguistic	*Gas* and *gasoline* refer to the same thing
	Factual	There are 100 cents in a dollar
	Schematic	This is a comparison problem
Solution	Strategic	The goals are to find the cost per gallon at Chevron and the total cost of gas at Chevron
	Procedural	Add .05 to 1.13; multiply 1.18 by 5

What is your diagnosis concerning our students' knowledge for mathematical problem solving? It appears that the students are having difficulty with the representation of word problems, because the wording of the problem seems to be a major factor in eliciting errors. What can be done to improve students' mathematical problem-solving performance? A straightforward implication is that some students may need training in how to represent the sentences of word problems. In particular, students need practice in how to represent relational statements such as, "This is 5 cents less per gallon than gas at Chevron." This recommendation is particularly important in light of the observation that most mathematics textbooks emphasize problem solution, whereas students' major difficulties occur in problem representation.

Representation Training

Lewis (1989, in press) developed a 2-hour training program to help students improve their problem representation skills for mathematical problem solving. Students learn to identify relational statements and to translate relational statements into diagrams using a number line. For example, the worksheet in Table 8 shows the procedure that students learn for translating sentences into diagrams. As you can see, the student receives practice in systematically translating sentences into diagrams rather than relying on keywords such as *more* or *less*.

Table 8
Example Worksheet for Representation Training

Problem: At ARCO gas sells for $1.13 per gallon. This is 5 cents less per gallon than gas at Chevron. How much does gas cost at Chevron?

Step 1: Locating known variable on number line

——————— X ———————
ARCO, $1.13

Step 2: Marking possible relationship of unknown to known variable

——— ? ——— X ——— ? ———
ARCO, $1.13

Step 3: Tentative placement of unknown variable

——— ? ——— X ——— ? ———
Chevron ARCO, $1.13

Step 4: Representation verification

——— ? ——— X ——— ? ———
Chevron ARCO, $1.13

ARCO is 5 cents less per gallon than gas at Chevron.
If verification is not found try other "?" and check again

——— ? ——— X ——— ? ———
ARCO, $1.13 Chevron

Step 5: Plan arithmetic operation

——— ? ——— X ——— ? ———
ARCO, $1.13 Chevron

→
addition
$1.13 + .05 = Chevron's price

Note. Adapted from Lewis (in press).

Like Cook's (1982) structure training, Lewis' representation training is consistent with each of the three characteristics of successful problem-solving programs described in the introduction of this paper. Representation training focuses on small component skills, namely, on strategies for how to recognize and represent relational statements. Furthermore, representation training relies on students learning to model the appropriate process, the systematic translation of sentences into diagrams. Finally, the training is part of a specific subject domain, the solving of word problems.

Evaluation of Representation Training

What are the effects of representation training? To answer this question, Lewis provided representation training to a group of college students who had trouble solving work problems. Before training, the students took a pretest that included two-step word problems like those shown in Table 6 as well as word problems that required three arithmetic steps, such as the following:

> Alfredo is 25 years old. He is 7 years younger than Pedro, who is 3 years older than Dennis. How old will Dennis be in 8 years?

After training, students took a posttest that included equivalent two-step and three-step word problems. A control group received practice in solving the same problems that the trained group solved but did not receive direction in how to represent problems. In both groups, the example problems required one or two steps but not three steps, so the two-step problems were considered retention problems and the three-step problems were considered transfer problems.

The bar graph in Figure 2 summarizes the pretest-to-posttest changes in error rates on solving two-step (retention) and three-step (transfer) word problems for the trained and control groups. For two-step (retention) problems, both groups averaged about the same number of errors on the pretest. Both groups showed a pretest-to-posttest improvement in solving two-step problems, although the trained group improved significantly more than the control group. For three-step (transfer) problems, both groups averaged about the same number of errors on the pretest. However, on the posttest, the trained group showed significant improvement in solving transfer problems, whereas the control group did not. In summary, the trained group displayed evidence of transfer to three-step problems, whereas the control group did not.

These results demonstrate that representation training can improve students' creative problem-solving transfer performance. Even though students were trained on two-step problems, they were able to

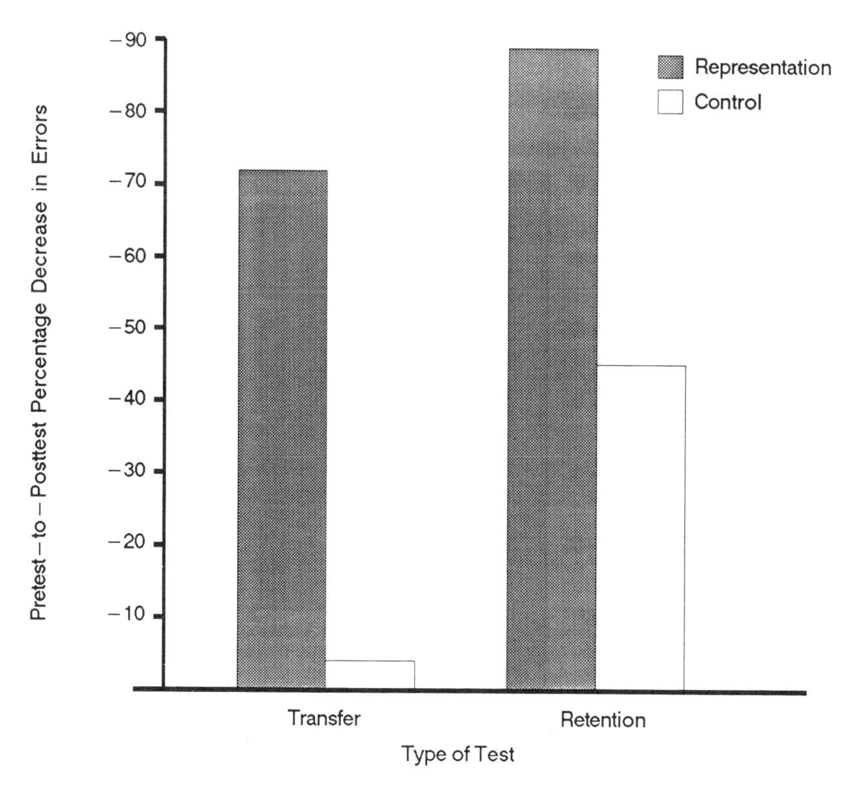

Figure 2. Pretest-to-posttest changes of representation trained and control groups. Adapted from Lewis (in press).

transfer what they had learned to a new problem situation, namely to three-step problems. The trained group's ability to transfer is consistent with the definition of meaningful learning outcomes described in the introduction. Apparently, representation training is another example of teaching for thinking.

The effectiveness of representation training may be limited by the characteristics of the learners. For example, the students in Lewis' study possessed good computational skills and good reading skills. If the students had not possessed these skills, it is unlikely that a small amount of representation training would have helped them. Similarly, although the students possessed good arithmetic and reading skills, they lacked experience in solving arithmetic word problems. If the students were already expert problem solvers, representation training would not have been needed for them. In short, representation training is likely to be most valuable for students who possess appropriate background skills in computation but who perform poorly on solving word problems.

Teaching for Thinking in Computer Programming

Issue

As a third example, suppose that students who have never had any experience in computer programming or high-level mathematics are given the opportunity to learn BASIC computer programming. Furthermore, assume that they participate in three sessions in which they read a standard BASIC manual and have hands-on experience with computers. In the training, they learn to use statements such as READ, DATA, INPUT, LET, PRINT, GOTO, IF, FOR, NEXT, and END.

When we test students on retention, requiring that they write grammatically correct statements or that they answer questions about simple facts from the manual, they perform well. For example, they are able to fill in the correct answer for the problem, "The computer will execute the statement following THEN only when the statement immediately following ____ is true." (The correct answer is IF.) When we test our students on transfer, requiring them to write or to comprehend short programs, they perform poorly. For example, they have difficulty explaining what the following program does:

```
10  INPUT A, B, C
20  LET D = A + B + C
30  D = D/3
40  PRINT D
50  END
```

This pattern of results was obtained in several studies (Bayman & Mayer, 1983, 1988).

What do students need to know to perform well on solving programming problems? Mayer (1988) identified four kinds of knowledge that may be required for successful problem solving in programming: syntactic, semantic, schematic, and strategic knowledge. *Syntactic knowledge* refers to knowledge of language features and to facts such as knowing that each line in a BASIC program must begin with a line number. *Semantic knowledge* (Mayer, 1985a) refers to a conceptual model of the computer system including the kinds of actions that can take place inside the computer (e.g., moving, erasing, copying), the kinds of locations in the computer (e.g., input queue, output screen, memory space), and the kinds of objects that can be acted on (e.g., numbers, program lines, pointers). *Schematic knowledge* refers to knowledge of program modules that carry out specific functions, such as modules for sorting data or for ordering data. *Strategic knowledge* refers to techniques for using syntactic, semantic, and schematic knowledge to develop and execute solution plans.

Because the students are in the preliminary phase of learning BASIC, we focus only on their acquisition of syntactic and semantic knowledge as summarized in Table 9. It appears from the students' performance that they retain the syntactic information from the manual but have difficulty transferring what they have learned to new problems. A straightforward diagnosis of their problem is that they have acquired syntactic knowledge but have not acquired appropriate semantic knowledge. To remediate this problem, the students may need training that emphasizes semantic knowledge along with syntactic knowledge. Thus, the students need help building conceptual

Table 9
Types of Knowledge Required for Computer Programming

Type of knowledge	Examples from BASIC
Syntactic knowledge	
Lexical Units	
Line numbers	10, 20, 30, 40
Keywords	LET, INPUT, PRINT, IF
Variable names	A, B, C
Numerical values	10.2, 5, −.322
Arithmetic symbols	+, −, *, /, **
Logical relations	=, >, <
Punctuation	(), ; : "
Combination Rules	
Micro-rules	For every (in a statement there must be a corresponding)
Macro-rules	A FOR statement on one line of a program requires a NEXT statement on a subsequent line
Semantic knowledge	
Microsemantics	
Actions	Move, find, create, destroy, decide, combine, wait, allow
Objects	Number, program line, pointer
Locations	Input queue, memory space, program list, output screen, keyboard
Macrosemantics	
Do-until loop	FOR—action—NEXT module
Ordering numbers	INPUT—IF—LET module
Manipulating data	INPUT—LET—PRINT module

Note. Adapted from Dyck and Mayer.

models of what goes on inside the computer when each statement is executed. Interestingly, most BASIC manuals emphasize appropriate grammar for each statement—the keyword READ must be preceded by a line number and a blank space and must be followed by a blank space and an address name or list—but barely touch on relevant conceptual models that a user might use to understand processes to which the statements refer.

Conceptual-Model Training

Bayman (1983; Bayman & Mayer, 1988) used conceptual-model training to help novice programmers understand what goes on inside the computer for each BASIC statement. She began with a standard BASIC manual that emphasized language syntax for each of ten BASIC statements; then, she inserted information about the conceptual model underlying each statement. For example, Table 10 provides a

Table 10
Example Sections for Concrete Model and Standard Manual

Introductory Text Common to Both Manuals for the LET Statement

In the memory of a computer there is a special area that is set aside to store values defined by the user. This area can be thought of as a group of memory spaces. Each memory space can contain *only one value at a time.* In most computer programming languages, the value of a variable (or a memory space) changes each time it is assigned a new value by the user. A value is assigned to a variable by using the LET statement. For practical reasons, all the variable names used throughout this minicourse will be letters of the alphabet.

Standard Manual

Now assume that you type in:

LET A = 1 and press the RETURN key.

The value 1 will be stored in variable A.

Concrete Model Manual

Now, assume that you type in:

LET A = 1 and press the RETURN key.

The steps the computer carries out are:

1. FIND the number stored in memory space A.
2. ERASE the number in memory space A.
3. WRITE the number 1 in memory space A.
4. WAIT FOR the next statement to be entered from the keyboard.

Note. Adapted from Bayman & Mayer (1988).

section of the standard manual along with the corresponding section of a conceptual-model manual. As you can see, the manuals are identical in their descriptions of language syntax for each statement, but the conceptual model includes additional information about the semantics of each statement. In particular, the conceptual-model manual lists the actions that are carried out on objects inside the computer for each statement.

The conceptual-model training is designed to help students acquire a conceptual model of the computer as shown in Figure 3. The model provides a concrete representation of several of the main functional locations in the computer, including an erasable memory scoreboard, a program list with pointer arrow, an output screen, an input queue with pointer arrow, a wait/run traffic light, and an erasable scratchpad for arithmetic computations. Similar models have been used in previous research (Mayer, 1981, in press).

Like structure training for scientific problem solving and representation training for mathematical problem solving, conceptual-model training is consistent with the three features of successful thinking-skills programs listed in the introduction of this paper. Conceptual-model training focuses on small component skills, that is, it translates each programming statement into a concrete description of actions inside the computer. Conceptual-model training emphasizes

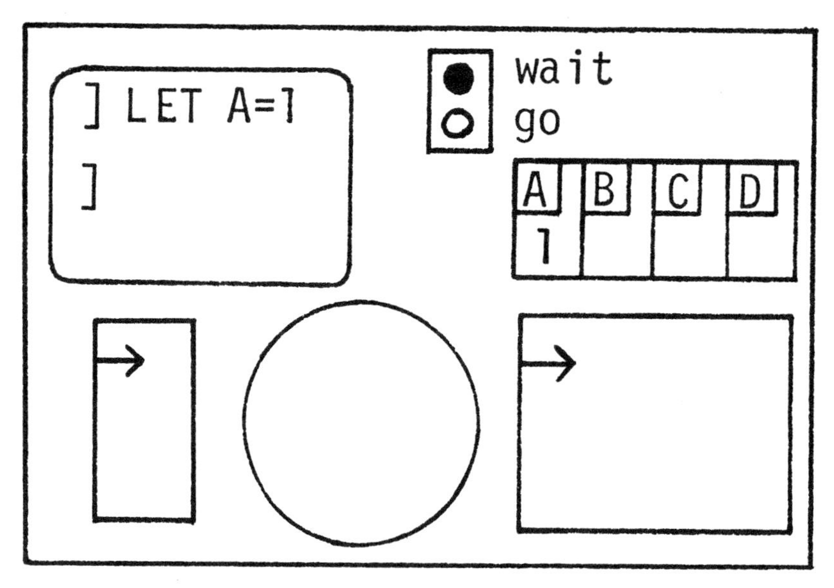

Figure 3. A conceptual model for learning BASIC computer programming. Adapted from Bayman and Mayer (1988).

process by systematically analyzing what each statement means. Finally, conceptual-model training embeds problem-solving training within the specific domain of computer programming.

Evaluation of Conceptual-Model Training

To evaluate the effectiveness of conceptual-model training, Bayman (1983; Bayman & Mayer, 1988) gave students a 2-hour introduction to BASIC computer programming using either a standard manual or a standard manual that was enhanced with conceptual training. After instruction, the students took retention tests, which evaluated whether they had acquired the syntactic knowledge in the standard manual and the semantic knowledge in the enhanced manual, and transfer tests to determine whether they could transfer what they had learned to solve new programming problems.

To evaluate syntactic knowledge, students were given fact-retention questions such as those previously described. This was considered a retention test because it covered material that was presented in the manual for both groups of students. To evaluate problem-solving transfer, students were asked to generate or interpret short BASIC programs such as those previously described. This was considered a transfer test because students were not explicitly trained in how to put statements together to solve programming problems.

Does conceptual-model training improve students' abilities to transfer what they have learned about the statements to new programming problems? The left portion of Figure 4 summarizes the performance of the standard and conceptual-model groups on retention and transfer tests. As expected, the groups did not differ on retention, but the conceptual-model group outperformed the standard group on problem-solving transfer. These results are consistent with the idea that conceptual-model training fosters the development of meaningful learning outcomes.

Does conceptual-model training improve students' semantic knowledge? To evaluate students' semantic knowledge, students were given lines of BASIC code such as "70 LET A = B + 1" and were asked to list "in plain English all of the steps that the computer has to carry out in order to execute this line." An answer was scored as correct if it contained the major actions underlying the statement, such as "replace the number in memory space A with the value of B + 1." As shown in the right portion of Figure 4, the conceptually trained students performed much better than the standard-trained students on tests of semantic knowledge. This finding helps to validate that conceptual-model training was successful in improving students' semantic knowledge.

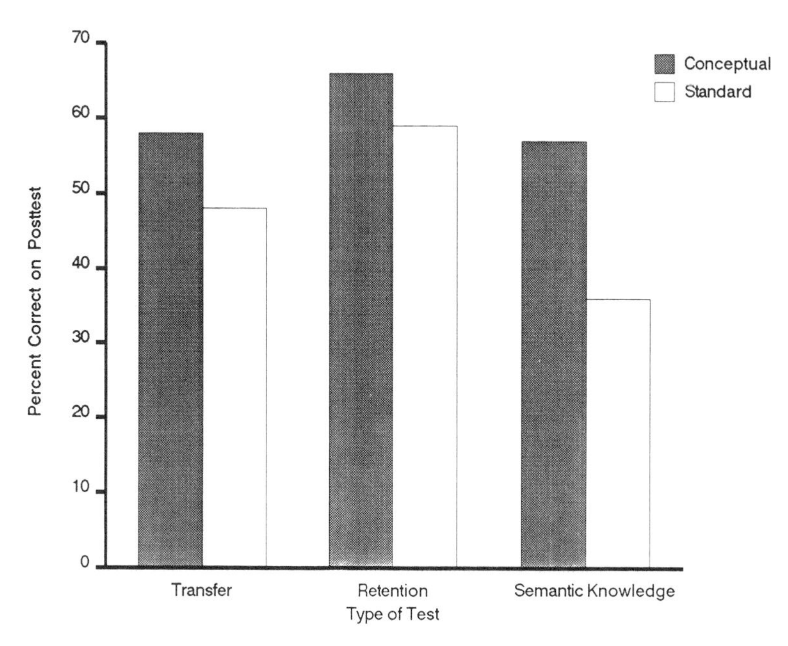

Figure 4. Posttest performance of conceptual-model trained and standard groups. (Data were collapsed across several versions of conceptual-model training.) Adapted from Bayman and Mayer (1988).

Finally, do students who possess good conceptual models of the computer transfer what they have learned better than students who possess poor models? To answer this question, Bayman compared students who scored high on the test of semantic knowledge with those who scored low. As expected, students with good conceptual models performed much better on the transfer test (75% correct) than those with poor conceptual models (42% correct). This finding helps to demonstrate a relation between acquiring underlying semantic knowledge and the ability to succeed on transfer.

In summary, conceptual-model training appears to be another example of teaching for thinking. Apparently, students who learn under this method develop conceptual models of the computer system that help them to transfer what they have learned to the solving of new programming problems. As in the previous exemplary training programs, the effectiveness of conceptual-model training may depend on learner characteristics. In particular, conceptual-model training is not effective with students who come to the classroom with strong backgrounds in mathematics and computer science. Presumably, these more able students already possess conceptual models to use in understanding new programming statements. In addition, research on expert/novice differences suggests that, as students become more expert in programming, the conceptual models used for initial training may need to be replaced with more sophisticated models (Mayer, in press).

Summary

In the introduction to this paper, I alluded to the disappointments awaiting anyone who wants to search for the teachable aspects of problem solving. In this context, I described three thinking-skills programs whose goals were fairly modest—to examine teaching for transfer within relatively restricted domains. Fortunately, several promising themes run through each of the exemplary thinking-skills programs that I have described.

First, this work demonstrates that it is possible to teach in a way that fosters students' thinking. Structure training, representation training, and conceptual-model training are all attempts at teaching for thinking. In each of the three programs, teaching for thinking succeeded in improving students' abilities to transfer what they had learned to new problem-solving situations.

Second, the common thread running through each of the programs is an emphasis on students' modeling of the comprehension process for problem solving in specific domains. In structure training, students learned to outline scientific text based on knowledge of typical expository prose structures. Knowing the basic kinds of text structures improved students' reading comprehension processes by allowing them to focus on important information and to organize the information in a way that allowed for inferences. In representation training, students learned how to translate mathematical word problems by using concrete diagrams. Knowing how to phrase the sentences in a word problem allowed students to focus on important information in the problem and to organize the information in a useful way. In conceptual-model training, students learned to translate programming statements into descriptions of what goes on inside the computer. Knowing how to use a conceptual model helped students to understand the relations among statements so they could generate and comprehend programs.

Third, although each training program emphasized comprehension processes, the traditional training for each subject area does not. Typically, students are not taught how to organize scientific text, how to translate word problems into diagrams, or how to build conceptual models for computer programming. Similarly, each of the training programs was intended to improve problem-solving transfer, whereas the traditional emphasis in many subject areas is on the retention of presented information. Thus, had we evaluated the effectiveness of our programs based solely on retention, we would not have found strong positive evidence. In short, the payoff for helping students become better comprehenders of problems lies in transfer rather than retention.

We are left with some tantalizing implications for anyone interested in research or practice in the teaching of thinking. Traditionally, educational programs have emphasized producing correct answers, whereas our research suggests that improvements in thinking are achieved through an emphasis on the processes by which answers are produced. Traditionally, improvements in intellectual performance have been attributed to the strengthening of some sort of monolithic ability, whereas our research suggests that improvements in thinking come about through instruction in small component intellectual skills such as comprehension processes. Finally, the teaching of thinking has sometimes been taught as a separate subject area, isolated from other subject areas, whereas the research on transfer suggests that we should integrate teaching for thinking into specific subject domains such as mathematics, science, or computer programming (Cormier & Hagman, 1987; Mayer, 1987b).

This chapter also suggests some ideas for anyone interested specifically in the teaching of thinking skills within the domain of psychology, although substantial research is needed to test these ideas. In general, critical thinking involves evaluating arguments; in psychology, arguments are generally supported by presenting empirical data, so the evaluation of arguments involves determining how well data support theories. Psychology students need practice in understanding arguments, critiquing arguments, and constructing arguments. Understanding arguments involves building a mental representation of relevant concepts, theories, predictions, and data. Students need practice in reading a textbook (or listening to a lecture) and determining the main concepts, definitions, examples, principles, theories, and supporting evidence. Critiquing arguments involves determining the degree to which a theory is supported by available data. Students need practice in identifying alternative interpretations and flaws in psychological arguments. Constructing arguments in psychology involves generating and testing hypotheses. Students need practice in aspects of generating hypotheses such as selecting definable concepts and deriving testable predictions; students also need practice in aspects of testing hypotheses such as collecting data and comparing data with predictions.

In conclusion, understanding how to accomplish teaching for thinking requires a fruitful interaction between those interested in developing psychological theories of human cognition and those interested in developing school curricula that serve the needs of our students. Questions about the teachability of thinking skills challenge researchers to develop a more complete understanding of the conditions that allow the transfer of problem-solving skills and challenge educators to develop a curriculum that has a place for thinking. In answering questions about the teachability of thinking skills, we can advance both our psychological theories of human problem solving and the educational practices of our schools. It is important that answers to these questions be based on solid research evidence and on well-documented psychological theories rather than on educational fads.

References

Bayman, P. (1983). *Effects of instructional procedures on learning a first programming language.* Unpublished doctoral dissertation, University of California, Santa Barbara.

Bayman, P., & Mayer, R. E. (1983). Diagnosis of beginning programmers' misconceptions of BASIC programming statements. *Communications of the ACM, 26,* 519–521.

Bayman, P., & Mayer, R. E. (1988). Using conceptual models to teach BASIC computer programming. *Journal of Educational Psychology, 80,* 291–298.

Cook, L. K. (1982). *Instructional effects of text structure-based reading strategies on the comprehension of scientific prose.* Unpublished doctoral dissertation, University of California, Santa Barbara.

Cook, L. K., & Mayer, R. E. (1988). Teaching readers about the structure of scientific text. *Journal of Educational Psychology, 80,* 448–456.

Cormier, S. M., & Hagman, J. D. (Eds.). (1987). *Transfer of learning: Contemporary research and applications.* San Diego, CA: Academic Press.

Detterman, D. K., & Sternberg, R. J. (Eds.). (1982). *How and how much can intelligence be increased.* Norwood, NJ: ABLEX.

Dyck, J. L., & Mayer, R. E. (1989). Teaching for transfer of computer program comprehension. *Journal of Educational Psychology, 81,* 16–24.

Lewis, A. B. (1989). *Effects of representation training on students' comprehension of relational statements in arithmetic word problems.* Unpublished doctoral dissertation, University of California, Santa Barbara.

Lewis, A. B. (in press). Training students to represent arithmetic word problems. *Journal of Educational Psychology.*

Lewis, A. B., & Mayer, R. E. (1987). Students' misconception of relational statements in arithmetic word problems. *Journal of Educational Psychology, 79,* 363–371.

Mayer, R. E. (1981). The psychology of how novices learn computer programming. *Computing Surveys, 13,* 121–141.

Mayer, R. E. (1982). Memory for algebra story problems. *Journal of Educational Psychology, 74,* 199–216.

Mayer, R. E. (1983). *Thinking, problem solving, cognition.* New York: Freeman.

Mayer, R. E. (1984). Aids to prose comprehension. *Educational Psychologist, 19,* 30–42.

Mayer, R. E. (1985a). Learning in complex domains: A cognitive analysis of computer programming. In G. Bower (Ed.), *Psychology of learning and motivation* (Vol. 19, pp. 89–130). New York: Academic Press.
Mayer, R. E. (1985b). Mathematical ability. In R. J. Sternberg (Ed.), *Human abilities: An information processing approach* (pp. 127–150). New York: Freeman.
Mayer, R. E. (1987a). *Educational psychology: A cognitive approach.* Boston: Little, Brown.
Mayer, R. E. (1987b). The elusive search for teachable aspects of problem solving. In J. A. Glover & R. R. Ronning (Eds.), *Historical foundations of educational psychology* (pp. 327–348). New York: Plenum Press.
Mayer, R. E. (1987c). Instructional variables that influence cognitive processing during reading. In B. K. Britton & S. Glynn (Eds.), *Executive control processes in reading* (pp. 127–216). Hillsdale, NJ: Erlbaum.
Mayer, R. E. (1988). From novice to expert. In M. Helendar (Ed.), *Handbook of human computer interaction* (Vol. 6, pp. 569–580). Amsterdam, The Netherlands: Elsevier.
Mayer, R. E. (in press). Models for understanding. *Review of Educational Research.*
Mayer, R. E., Larkin, J. H., & Kadane, J. B. (1984). A cognitive analysis of mathematical problem solving ability. In R. J. Sternberg (Ed.), *Advances in the psychology of human intelligence* (Vol. 2, pp. 321–373). Hillsdale, NJ: Erlbaum.
Nickerson, R. W., Perkins, S. N., & Smith, E. E. (Eds.). (1985). *The teaching of thinking.* Hillsdale, NJ: Erlbaum.
Segal, J. W., Chipman, S. F., & Glaser, R. (Eds.). (1985). *Thinking and learning skills: Volume 1. Relative instruction to research.* Hillsdale, NJ: Erlbaum.